TWAYNE'S WORLD AUTHORS SERIES

A Survey of the World's Literature

Sylvia E. Bowman, Indiana University
GENERAL EDITOR

FRANCE

Maxwell A. Smith, Guerry Professor of French, Emeritus
The University of Chattanooga
Visiting Professor in Modern Languages
The Florida State University
EDITOR

Madame de Lafayette

(TWAS 90)

TWAYNE'S WORLD AUTHORS SERIES (TWAS)

The purpose of TWAS is to survey the major writers —novelists, dramatists, historians, poets, philosophers, and critics—of the nations of the world. Among the national literatures covered are those of Australia, Canada, China, Eastern Europe, France, Germany, Greece, India, Italy, Japan, Latin America, New Zealand, Poland, Russia, Scandinavia, Spain, and the African nations, as well as Hebrew, Yiddish, and Latin Classical literatures. This survey is complemented by Twayne's United States Authors Series and English Authors Series.

The intent of each volume in these series is to present a critical-analytical study of the works of the writer; to include biographical and historical material that may be necessary for understanding, appreciation, and critical appraisal of the writer; and to present all material in clear, concise English—but not to vitiate the scholarly content of the work by doing so.

Madame de Lafayette

By STIRLING HAIG

University of North Carolina

Twayne Publishers, Inc.   ::   New York

FOR MY FAMILY

MANUFACTURED IN THE UNITED STATES OF AMERICA

Preface

I shall not pretend that this study is addressed to the general reader. This is not because I disdain him, but rather because I have never been able to determine the "general" reader's identity, or guess at his whereabouts. In fact, his very existence has always seemed mythical to me. At the very least, I certainly doubt that he exists as a potential audience for this book.

My study is therefore intended for an educated reader who is not necessarily a specialist in French literature. I have assumed that this reader has some slight prior knowledge of Madame de Lafayette and her century, or interest in her works that has led him to this book. I have further assumed that even well-informed readers know Madame de Lafayette only through *La Princesse de Clèves* and that a certain amount of summarizing was thus called for in my examination of her lesser works. By the same token, I felt that less summarizing was necessary in the chapter devoted to her masterpiece. Because of the length of *La Princesse de Clèves* and because of space limitations, I have not attempted to deal with every detail of this novel and have oriented my discussion toward what I call its "inwardness." There is not a separate chapter on Madame de Lafayette's historical writings. Their interest being chiefly biographical, I have incorporated a discussion of them into the first chapter.

Madame de Lafayette, like all seventeenth-century French authors, is very hard to translate into English; moreover, Madame de Lafayette herself is hardly a paragon of stylistic elegance or even grammatical correctness. Nevertheless, the translations are mine, and I accept full responsibility for their shortcomings. Balzac, Stendhal, even Proust himself have met with objections of a stylistic nature from their critics; and yet the very power of their writing has disarmed such strictures. The same is true of Mme de Lafayette.

Acknowledgments

This is the first book on all Madame de Lafayette's works to appear in English in over fifty years. In English, I hasten to emphasize, for the interest of the French has never flagged, as the reader will note from my frequent references to French critics in the footnotes. Where credit is due, I have given it.

I am greatly indebted, particularly in Chapter 1, to André Beaunier and Emile Magne, especially the latter's two-volume biography of Madame de Lafayette. I have not always agreed with M. Magne's conclusions, but I must pay tribute to his great scholarly genius. I think no man could breathe more life into the dry and dusty documents of scholarship than he was able to.

I am grateful to the Princeton University Committee on Research in the Humanities and Social Sciences for a grant that enabled me to carry out a portion of my research at the Bibliothèque Nationale, and to the Smith Fund Committee of the University of North Carolina for assistance in the preparation of my typescript. I must also thank the late Professor E. B. O. Borgerhoff of Princeton and Professor W. L. Wiley of North Carolina for their time and suggestions. Finally, my greatest thanks go to my most persistent and vexing critic, my wife, whose contributions to the writing of this study were invaluable.

Contents

Chronology

1633   Marriage of Marc Pioche, Sieur de la Vergne (gentleman of minor nobility) and Isabelle Pena, at the Church of Saint-Sulpice.

1634   (March 18) Baptism of Marie-Madeleine, Pioche de La Vergne in Saint-Sulpice. Godparents: Urbain de Maillé and the Duchesse d'Aiguillon.
Marc Pioche begins construction of a house at the corner of the Rue Férou and the Rue de Vaugirard (n° 50 today) that will become Mme de Lafayette's residence in 1658.

1648   Beginning of the Fronde. Isabelle Pena and her daughters go to Le Havre, where M. de La Vergne is lieutenant governor.

1649   (December) Death of Marc Pioche de La Vergne.

1650   (December) Isabelle Pena is wed to Renaud-René de Sévigné (uncle by marriage of the Marquise de Sévigné). During the Fronde, he commanded the *régiment de Corinthe,* raised by the Cardinal de Retz. Marie-Madeleine becomes *demoiselle d'honneur* of the Queen and meets Ménage, Retz's secretary.

1652   Renaud-René, compromised in the Fronde, is ordered to withdraw to his estate at Champiré (in Anjou). Marie-Madeleine meets Mme de Sévigné.

1652–54 Visits to Paris during which Marie-Madeleine meets, in the Convent of Chaillot, her future sister-in-law and Henriette d'Angleterre. She reads *Le Grand Cyrus* and the first volume of *Clélie,* sent to her by Ménage.

1655   (Feb. 15) She marries, in Saint-Sulpice, Jean-François Motier, Comte de Lafayette. Born in 1616, he is a widower and the brother of Mère Angélique of the Visitandines, the former platonic love of Louis XIII.

1656 Death of Isabelle Pena.

1658 (March 7) Baptism of Mme de Lafayette's first son, Louis, future Abbé de Valmont, de Dallon, de la Grenetière, who dies on May 12, 1729. Ill, Mme de Lafayette takes a cure at Vichy.

1659 Mme de Lafayette meets Huet and Segrais. She publishes her first and only signed literary effort, a portrait of Mme de Sévigné in Mademoiselle's *Divers Portraits.* (Sept. 17) Birth of Armand de Lafayette, future soldier of the King who will die at Landau on Aug. 12, 1694.

1661 Henriette d'Angleterre marries Monsieur, Louis XIV's brother. Mme de Lafayette has entrée to the Court. Mazarin dies. Fouquet is arrested. M. de Lafayette returns alone to Auvergne.

1662 Publication of *La Princesse de Montpensier.* Mme de Lafayette frequents the society of the Du Plessis-Guénégauds where she is known as the *nymphe de l'Allier.* She meets La Rochefoucauld.

1664 Publication of La Rochefoucauld's *Maximes.*

1665 Beginning of her friendship with La Rochefoucauld. She begins writing her *Histoire d'Henriette d'Angleterre.*

1669 Ménage ceases his relations with Mme de Lafayette. With La Rochefoucauld and Segrais she composes *Zaïde,* the first volume of which is published under Segrais' name in 1670

1670 Death of Madame. Publication of Pascal's *Pensées.*

1670–71 Publication of the second volume of *Zaïde.*

1672 Mme de Lafayette probably begins work on *La Princesse de Clèves.* Long source readings (histories and court ceremonials) interrupted by illness, death, mourning, lawsuits.

1675 Mme de Lafayette becomes a diplomatic agent for the Duchesse de Savoie (Jeanne-Baptiste de Nemours) whom she knew at Chaillot. Mme de Villedieu publishes *Les Désordres de l'amour.*

1678 (March 17) *La Princesse de Clèves* goes on sale. Donneau de Visé's *Mercure Galant* asks for its readers' reactions. Valincour's critique, *Lettres à Mme la marquise de * * * sur le sujet de la Princesse de Clèves* is published. Boursault puts on a stage version of *La Princesse de Clèves.*

1679 With the probable collaboration of Mme de Lafayette, the Abbé de Charnes publishes a countercritique, *Conversations sur la critique de la Princesse de Clèves.*

1680 La Rochefoucauld dies, with Bossuet in attendance.

1683 Death of M. de Lafayette.

1684 Mme de Lafayette and Ménage reconciled.

1692 Death of Ménage.

1693 (May 25) Death of Mme de Lafayette; her funeral is held two days later at Saint-Sulpice.

1720 Publication of the *Histoire d'Henriette d'Angleterre.*

1724 Publication of *La Comtesse de Tende.*

1731 Publication of the *Mémoires de la Cour de France pour les années 1688 & 1689*

Several other works come to light posthumously have been attributed to Mme de Lafayette. The *Mémoires de Hollande,* it is now agreed, are from the pen of Courtilz de Sandras. The *Histoire Espagnole* and *Histoire de Don Carlos d'Astorgas* are certainly not by her, nor is the unpublished *Caraccio.* The attribution to Mme de Lafayette of *Le Triomphe de l'indifférence* is at best doubtful, and that of *Isabelle ou le Journal Amoureux* erroneous.

CHAPTER 1

"It is enough to be"

I *Love and Reason*

In 1653, at the age of nineteen years, Mademoiselle Marie-Madeleine, Pioche de La Vergne, wrote to her friend Gilles Ménage: "I am so convinced that love is a bothersome thing that I am glad that I and my friends are exempt from it" (C I, 34).[1] Little more than a year later, in the church of Saint-Sulpice, the same young Parisienne was married to Jean-François Motier, Comte de Lafayette,[2] a provincial nobleman and widower of nearly twice her age. Given the unfavorable opinion she held of love, what can she have thought of this marriage? Young girls of her day were not consulted in these matters, any more than the seventeenth-century youth who asked, "Is it true, father, that you plan to marry me to Mademoiselle so-and-so?"—"Son, mind your own business."[3]

The couple traveled to the Count's domains in the misty and mountainous Auvergne, where the young Countess read fashionable novels, entertained provincial nobility, and interested herself in her husband's tangled lawsuits. Mme de Lafayette was apparently doomed to the lonely life of a châtelaine in one of France's dreariest provinces.

The Motier de Lafayette were a family of glorious ancestry who could trace their forebears to the eleventh century. They had taken part in the crusades under Saint Louis, fought with Joan of Arc at Orléans and Compiègne, been Senechals of the Bourbonnais and Knights of Malta, grand squires and chamberlains of the Kings of France. Little by little, however, their race became less martial, knew reduced but never penurious circumstances, and more and more led the glum existence of provincial nobility. Too many sons divided the patrimony, too many daughters needed dowries, and too few advantageous matches—financially speaking—were contracted. The family estates were encumbered with debts and mired in litigations that had been continuing for nearly two generations by 1655. François de Lafayette's lawsuits, by the time he remarried, had become the principal distraction and distress of his hermitic existence in Auvergne. Deeply attached to his domains and ill at ease in the capital, he settled with his new Countess in the Château de Nades. Could the couple have loved each other? There is only one document where Mme de Lafayette speaks of her husband and her life in the provinces. It is a letter addressed to Ménage, and dates from Sept. 1, 1656:

Since I last wrote you I have been on a continual round of visits. M. de Bayard was one of them, and if I told you the others you would not be better informed: they are people that you have the good fortune not to know, and I the misfortune of having as neighbors. Nonetheless, I must admit to the shame of my delicacy that I am not bored with these people, although they are hardly entertaining. But I have adopted a certain way of talking to them of things they know that keeps me from being bored.

It is also true that we have some men hereabouts who have fine minds, for provincials. The women are far from being so reasonable; but then they scarcely pay any visits, and so one is not bothered with them. For my part, I much prefer to see hardly any people at all than to see bothersome ones, and my solitude here is more pleasant than boring. Household cares busy and amuse me greatly; and, moreover, as I have no troubles, as my husband adores me, as I love him greatly [je l'aime fort], as I am my absolute mistress, I assure you that the life I lead is a very happy one and that I only ask God to continue it. When one believes one is happy, you know that that suffices to be so, and as I am convinced that I am happy, I live more contentedly than perhaps all the Queens of Europe. (C I, 68–69)

There is a hint of resignation and "making the best of

things" in this letter. Mme de Lafayette hardly found the provinces amusing—she once described Auvergne as being as remote and hidden as the state of Tartary (C I, 55)—and her health was not good. As for her feelings for her husband, the nuance one attributes to the adverb *fort* is important. Did she love him "a great deal" or "a good deal"? In any case she does not say that she "adored" him as he adored her. Despite letters from her friend Ménage, the books he sent her, and the literary disputes he informed her of, she felt cut off. She complained that lawyering so occupied her that she had no time for "poetry, Italian, or Spanish" and could no longer think of herself as a *bel esprit.*[4] And despite her protestation of love for M. de Lafayette, she was soon to be separated from him. By 1659, she had suffered a miscarriage and given birth to two sons. Both spouses sojourned in Paris that year, but in 1660 M. de Lafayette returned alone to Auvergne. Monsieur had land to care for; Madame had children to educate. Moreover, her contacts in Paris permitted her to look after the family lawsuits (M I, 240–41).[5] Little by little, it was tacitly understood that the wife would continue to live in the capital and that the husband would come to see her from time to time.[6] There is nowhere any mention of a quarrel that might explain the separation, and we can only speculate that this curious arrangement, if not ideal, was convenient and suited them both. This *mariage de raison* was also a reasonable marriage. M. de Lafayette reappears now and again, but Mme de Lafayette's destiny is henceforth quite distinct from his.

In Paris, Mme de Lafayette continued what were to be her lifelong activities as business woman, furthering her husband's affairs in the courts, exerting influence for her sons' careers, and becoming widely acquainted with *la cour et la ville*: she came to know the great and the small, from Louis XIV to the obscure Dutch visitors who were flattered to visit this *"précieuse* of the highest rank." She was often praised for her qualities of mind: Costar called her a "fine wit"; Ménage celebrated, in Italian, her *purgato giudizio;* Mme de Sévigné singled out her "divine reason"; and La Rochefoucauld, who found little evidence of sincerity in mankind, paid her the highest compliment of all in terming her *vraie*. A reasonable woman, then, and a woman of reason, a tough-minded woman of businesslike sobriety who had carefully observed (and recorded) the intrigues and jealousies of a court whose principal occupation under the young Louis—not yet the bigoted and vainglorious Sun King—was love, or at least romance. She saw the tragic death of her girlhood friend, Henrietta of England (poisoned, she believed); the insane jealousy of that lady's husband, Monsieur, "only brother of the King"; the follies of the romantic Guiche; and the philanderings of the King himself. She was a reserved and distant young woman (at the Hôtel de Nevers she was called *le brouillard*—the "fog") who left, no doubt, the impression of a placid languorousness. No intellectual precocity foreshadows her career as the greatest novelist of her century. (Ménage, one of her closest acquaintances, never knew until two years before her death that she was the author of *La Princesse de Clèves.*) No confidences betray her penetration and powers of observation; her personality lies in the shadow of her mind. She preserved throughout her life this aristocratic reticence that was dignity rather than haughtiness. But posterity will never know her heart. She was, and would remain, an eminently private person, who summed up her thoughts on life in one astonishingly stark aphorism: *"C'est assez que d'être"*— "It is enough to be." [7]

Her century held love and reason as antithetical, and it is not surprising that the "reasonable" Mme de Lafayette, already predisposed as a young girl against love, should compose an "Argument Against Love (C I, 192–93) or that she should secretly write novels in which she laid bare what she thought were the terrible truths of passion. Yet as Pascal wrote, the heart has its reasons that reason does not know; and an older and wiser Mme de Lafayette asked in 1679, "at what age and in what time is one safe from love, especially when one has experienced its spell? One forgets the pain that follows and only remembers the pleasure, and resolutions vanish" (C II, 68–69). And to write against love is to write of it, to engage in that science of the heart in which her age excelled.

In Mme de Lafayette's works love is axiomatically a rejection of will and reason, and ultimately a betrayal of self. Fashioned by generations of Romantics and post-Romantics, our sensibilities and intelligence are no longer attuned to a sincerity of conduct—like the Princesse de Clèves'—that is anything but surrender to emotion, to "natural" impulses; indeed, the very sign of their authenticity is that they are repressed or "frustrated" by will, that social and therefore unnatural construct of the mind.[8] But Mme de Lafayette harbored a will to lucidity and self-possession through analysis that to her was not opposed to nature. Her works express a viewpoint more in accord with Descartes' *Traité des passions de l'âme* than Freud's psychoanalytical writings. Her heroines have self-knowledge imposed upon them, and seek *repos*, an elusive inward serenity; if they learn that love is an illusion, such lucidity does not bring happiness. Still the demand for clarity is imperious.

II *Youth*

The woman whom Louis XIV personally escorted in his carriage on a tour of Versailles was born of very minor nobility in 1634. Her father's only title at this time was *écuyer* (squire), and her mother's was simply *demoiselle*. Marc Pioche, Sieur de La Vergne, a cultured military engineer of undistinguished career, had lost his first wife and married Isabelle Pena in 1633, at which time he had become the governor of Richelieu's nephew, the Marquis de Brézé, and lived in the Petit Luxembourg palace. Here Mlle de La Vergne was born. Her godmother, Mme Combalet, the future Duchesse d'Aiguillon and niece of Richelieu, was a woman in whom the future author of *La Princesse de Clèves* might take some interest. In love with a certain Béthune, she had been forced to give him up for M. Combalet. After her husband's death, she inexplicably refused to marry Béthune.

Marc Pioche soon purchased a property near the Petit Luxembourg and began construction of a house on the Rue de Vaugirard that was to become Mme de Lafayette's in 1658. Here he received a distinguished intellectual company that included Pascal's father, the mathematician Jacques Le Pailleur, and men of letters such as Voiture, Chapelain, and the Abbé d'Aubignac. Two more daughters, Eléonor-Armande and Isabelle-Louise, were born to M. and Mme de La Vergne. They played absolutely no role in the life of Mme de Lafayette and, following the custom of undowried girls, entered a convent upon their father's death.

Meanwhile Marc Pioche went to war, first as engineer for the fortification of the town of Pontoise, threatened by the Spanish in 1636, later as a member of the mopping-up operations against the same Spanish in Picardy. He further accompanied his ward, the young Marquis de Brézé, in naval operations against the Spanish in 1640, and became lieutenant-governor of Le Havre in 1645. The Fronde, France's tragi-comic civil war, broke out in 1648, and Marc Pioche played his small role in it, expelling the rebel troops to whom nearby Harfleur had fallen. In 1649, he died. Of these fifteen years of Mme de Lafayette's youth, virtually nothing is known. There is one glimpse of her as a very young and playful child, who liked to throw a wrap over her head and "play the wolf" (M I, 19).

About the time of her father's death, Marie-Madeleine's literary education, such as it was, can be said to have commenced. There was no question, of course, of formal training, but rather the acquisition of social ease and urbanity through the frequentation of good society. There one could meet poets, scholars, and *literati* among people reputed for their fine wit. The young girl visited the Hôtel de Rambouillet—in its declining years, to be sure, for Julie d'Angennes was gone and the Fronde was in progress, but she met there her dearest friend, the person she said she most truly loved (C II, 218), the beautiful and witty Marquise de Sévigné. As for formal education, she probably had some spelling lessons—to judge by her letters she must have been a poor student—and some Italian, spoken by nearly all polite society in the seventeenth century. She visited also the celebrated Mlle de Scudéry, whose voluminous *roman à clef, Le Grand Cyrus,* was just beginning to appear. There she met the Abbé Gilles Ménage, a former visitor to her own family who was now attached to the Bishop Coadjutor of Paris, later Cardinal de Retz, and key figure in the Fronde.

In the meantime, in her own home, Widow La Vergne began to receive the Chevalier Renaud-René de Sévigné, a somewhat discredited Frondeur, uncle by marriage of the Marquise de Sévigné, who was sometimes accompanied by Monsignor Retz. If we can believe one contemporary source,[9] Marie-Madeleine thought that Renaud-René's attentions were for her and was disappointed to learn that the cavalier was interested in her mother. Their marriage was celebrated in Saint-Sulpice just a year after Marc Pioche's death. The former Isabelle Pena, *demoiselle,* could feed her vanity on her newly found title of *baronne* and soon pushed her husband to usurp the title of *marquis.* Thus was she consoled, for Renaud-René's implication in the Fronde earned him, in 1652, banishment to his estate at Champiré. Marie-Madeleine was consoled by gaining the entrée to the Louvre; through her godmother, the Duchesse d'Aiguillon, she joined Anne of Austria's ladies-in-waiting. This was her first introduction to court life, and she must have had to move delicately, for as the Regent Queen's maid of honor, she was also the stepdaughter of a Frondeur who was in turn a close acquaintance of the scheming Retz. But no one probably paid much attention to a seventeen-year old girl. These were turbulent times, and we find their echoes, transposed as the religious dissensions of the sixteenth century, in Mme de Lafayette's novels. Her literary apprenticeship had begun.

No suitors appear to have sought the somewhat masculine charms of Mlle de La Vergne, and this is perhaps why she did not send packing Gilles Ménage, *abbé galant,* poet and pedant, who was soon composing verse decrying her indifference and cruelty to him. While she did nothing to encourage his infatuation, neither did she do anything that might be construed as a definitive rebuff. Ménage might have been ridiculous and pedantic, but he was widely known, and all in all, his published poems were flattering to the young girl's reputation. And Ménage was a scholar: he had published an etymological dictionary and was particularly interested in Italian language and literature. In 1655 he published a commentary of the *Aminta;* later he became a member of the Accademia della Crusca and author of a study entitled *Origini della lingua italiana.* From 1672 to 1676 he published his *Observations sur la langue française.* Longuerue briefly paints him as the house buffoon of the Cardinal de Retz, throwing himself at the ladies' feet and wailing that although he had seen the word *brocanteur* (second-hand dealer) come into usage, he would probably die without having been able to discover its etymology. When someone was introduced, Longuerue says, Ménage would ask: "Is he a Hellenist?" (*Longueruana,* 23, 199) He was also a literary mystifier and plagiarist (M I, 146, 177) and served as model for Molière's pedantic Vadius in *Les Femmes Savantes.* Among women, Ménage had the reputation of a *patineur,* a name then given to men who had the annoying habit of pressing ladies' hands with a palpitating grasp while conversing with them.

This clownish figure nevertheless played a part of considerable importance during Marie-Madeleine's formative years. He taught her some Latin and Italian, introduced her to Petrarch, Tasso, and probably Virgil. While she was at Champiré, he procured copies of *Le Grand Cyrus* and *Clélie* for her. He was, after a fashion, her literary initiator, but nothing more, the famous *Carte de Tendre* of *Clélie* leaving her unimpressed. Finally, Ménage left in a sulk for the Maine and refused to correspond. Marie-Madeleine wrote that she was ill with fevers, and our poet immediately responded with an elegy wherein we find these verses:

> L'orgueilleuse Philis brûle enfin à son tour!
> Elle brûle, il est vrai, mais ce n'est pas d'amour.

Meanwhile Retz had been imprisoned in the Château de Nantes, not far from Champiré, and Renaud-René took his wife and stepdaughter to see him. Retz found Mme de Sévigné to be a "scheming" woman, easy to draw into a plot, and recorded this impression of her daughter: "She was quite pretty and pleasant. . . . I liked her a great deal, but the truth is that she liked me hardly at all' (*Mémoires*, II, xlii). Sévigné, with two accomplices, decided to arrange Retz's escape. They were successful, and all fled to Belle-Isle on August 16, 1654, only to find themselves invested. The Cardinal managed to escape again, but his friends were left behind and exposed to the threat of having their houses razed and their properties confiscated. Mother and daughter hastily returned to Paris to solicit the Duchesse d'Aiguillon's influence in the foolhardy Chevalier's behalf and to cultivate influential *dévotes*, those pious ladies whose sway was so often felt in court.

Thus nearing her majority with no husband in view, Marie-Madeleine had already considerable experience of life. She had known civil war, political chicanery, life at court, and *galanterie* (even if the *galant* happened to be Ménage); she had some acquaintance with literature and men of letters and had frequented polite society.

During these years Marie-Madeleine made her first visits to the Convent of the Visitation in Chaillot (on the present emplacement of the Palais de Chaillot), where lived Henriette-Marie de France, impoverished widow of the executed Charles I of England, and daughter of Henri IV and Marie de Médicis.

She resided there in humble circumstances with her young daughter Henriette-Anne Stuart, who was known as Henriette d'Angleterre, and with Visitandine nuns living under the rule of Saint François de Sales. Their future mother superior was Louise-Angélique de Lafayette, Marie-Madeleine's future sister-in-law, a timorous virgin who had fled the equally timorous advances of the little virile Louis XIII and taken the veil in 1637. The abbess had a widowed brother; Marie-Madeleine had no prospects; a marriage was arranged.

More important than her marriage, for us, was her nascent friendship with ten-year-old Henriette d'Angleterre. We will have more to say of this later, for in 1661 when Henriette became *Madame* (as the wife of *Monsieur* was quite logically called), Mme de Lafayette accompanied her to court as friend and confidante. Henriette's flirtatious conduct and ill-fated end confirmed Mme de Lafayette's prejudiced views of love and dangerous liaisons, and made of her a novelist who could inform fiction with the stuff of experienced reality, her greatest accomplishment and contribution to the progress of Classical prose. And Mme de Lafayette's description of Henriette's last hours, recorded in her *Relation de la mort de Madame,* is a great masterpiece of reporting, movingly told with the objective accuracy of true compassion.

III *Literary Debuts*

Conversation in the house on the Rue Férou was soon enlivened by two minor literary figures, Pierre-Daniel Huet and Jean-Regnauld de Segrais. Ménage introduced them. Huet was a man of humanist accomplishments in the Renaissance manner. He was a Latinist, a Hellenist, a student of Hebrew and mathematics, physics and philosophy, chemistry and law. Segrais, translator of the *Aeneid,* was a "romanist" (novelist) whose *Nouvelles Françoises,* published in 1656, were highly influential in the shaping of Mme de Lafayette's talents as novelist. He took an active part in the composition of *Zaïde,* which was published under his name. In 1659 he was in the service of the Duchesse de Montpensier, renowned for her heroics in the Fronde (La Rochefoucauld probably owed his life to her), and known simply as *Mademoiselle,* or sometimes, because of her height, as *la Grande Mademoiselle.*

Huet and Segrais were engaged in preparing for Mademoiselle a collection of literary portraits of the sort made fashionable by *Clélie,* to which illustrious personages were invited to contribute. They asked Mme de Lafayette, who chose to write a portrait of Mme de Sévigné. Eschewing physical description, Mme de Lafayette significantly strove to present her friend's inner qualities. In the *Divers Portraits* (as the collection was entitled), one learned nothing of the blonde Marquise's charms, but much of her virtue and lofty sentiments: "joy," she wrote of her friend, "is the true state of your soul." Readers could also find, in the same volume, the self-portrait of La Rochefoucauld. It was his first publication as well.

This first effort was probably revised and combed for style by the editors; at least they took the strange liberty of entitling it "Portrait of the Marquise de Sévigné by the Comtesse de Lafayette under the name of an unknown person." It was the first and only published writing of Mme de Lafayette's lifetime that gave her name as author. In the future she took careful steps to preserve her anonymity.

Meanwhile, Henriette d'Angleterre, her brother having been restored to the English throne, had become a considerable match, and was duly wed to the King's brother, Philippe, Duc d'Orléans, "the most delicious creature in France." The seventeen-year-old bride had little physical beauty—two contemporaries say she was slightly hunchbacked—but she exuded a delicate and evanescent charm that almost everyone was sensible of. Her friend Daniel de Cosnac wrote: "She blended in all her conversation a sweetness that could not be found in all the other royal persons. It was not that she had less majesty; but she knew how to make use of it in an easier and more touching manner, so that with so many wholly divine qualities, she did not fail to be the most human woman on earth. One would have said that she appropriated people's hearts to herself . . ." (HHA, 12).[10]

The English Princess had not forgotten Mme de Lafayette, and loved her for qualities "so serious in appearance that it did not seem they could please a Princess as young as Madame" (HHA, 38–39). "When she was married," wrote Mme de Lafayette in the preface of her *Histoire d'Henriette d'Angleterre,*

I had the entrée to her company, and although I was ten years older than she, she showed unto death much kindness and many considerations for me. She did not confide certain affairs to me, but when they were past, and almost become public, she took pleasure in telling me them.

In 1665, the Comte de Guiche was exiled. One day when she was telling me some rather extraordinary circumstances of his love for her, she said: "Do you not think, if all that has happened to me and its related circumstances were written down, it would make a pretty story? You write well," she added; "Write, and I shall provide you with some good memoirs." (HHA, 20–21) [11]

What the Princess had not guessed was that Mme de Lafayette had already drawn on her court experiences in writing her short novel *La Princesse de Montpensier* in 1662, nor that this story was largely an imaginative transposition of Madame's passion for Guiche. And to the extent that the novel was inspired by Madame's adventures, neither woman could know how ominously prophetic its ending was: the heroine dies "in the flower of her age, one of the most beautiful princesses on earth, who would no doubt have been the happiest, if virtue and prudence had guided her actions."

The analogies between Madame's life and this fiction are numerous and, following Emile Magne and André Beaunier, [12] let us briefly summarize them: Mlle de Mézières (maiden name of the Princesse de Montpensier), like Madame, appeared suddenly and triumphantly at court after having spent her youth elsewhere. Madame married Monsieur, but had eyes for his brother, the King, and Mlle de Mézières marries Montpensier while secretly loving the Duc de Guise. Madame despaired of Louis XIV's interest in Mlle de La Vallière, and Mlle de Mézières is jealous of Guise's attentions for Marguerite de Valois. Montpensier's jealousy resembles that of Monsieur, and the temerious Guise's secret rendezvous with the Princesse de Montpensier recalls Guiche's narrow escape one time when Monsieur unexpectedly arrived in Madame's apartments.

Madame's fancy soon passed, only to return four years later when she again urged Mme de Lafayette to write her memoirs. [13] They set about it seriously; Mme de Lafayette would transcribe what Madame had told her in the evening, and mornings they would revise it together. It was a difficult task, wrote Mme de Lafayette, "to turn the truth in certain places in such a way as to make it known without being offensive or unpleasant to the Princess." Problems of delicacy such as these were solved by omission—for the unsaid is a corollary of the impersonality of Classical prose—or by understatment, as in this discreet allusion to Monsieur's peculiar penchant: ". . . the miracle of enflaming this Prince's heart was reserved to no woman on earth" (HHA, 36).

But no matter how strong the echoes of Madame's imprudence and Guiche's follies in *La Princesse de Montpensier*, the true significance of the years Mme de Lafayette spent in the Palais-Royal lies in the observation of patterns of human behavior in love. They become not the events, but the structure and modality of her fictional works. While the tangled relationships that she follows in the *Histoire d'Henriette d'Angleterre* are much too complicated to summarize here, the reader may gain an idea of the intensity of intrigue and interest described by considering this: Madame, having already been the object of Buckingham's love in England, aspired to the heart of Louis XIV. He noticed her only after her marriage to his brother. When courtiers murmured, the King pretended to court Mlle de La Vallière, and his feigned affection began to seem only too genuine to Madame. Then Guiche, formerly the suitor of La Vallière, fell in love with Madame and found himself ill-served by his best friend Vardes, also in love with her. And very much in the foreground was the prancing Monsieur, who cared little for his wife, but whose violent jealousy the Queen Mother constantly played upon with hints and insinuations. Our historian's disillusioned reflections, despite her objective tone, are not hard to discern in phrases like these: "Time, absence, and reason finally made the King neglect his promise"; "Affection for a wife is rarely an obstacle to the love that one has for a mistress"; and of Vardes she wrote: "Madame did not rebuff him entirely; it is difficult to mistreat an agreeable confidant when the lover is absent" (HHA, 63).

Mme de Lafayette learned that the court game of sentimental hide-and-seek was a metaphor for duplicity, and the interplay of appearance and reality a parable of self-deception and self-knowledge. The birth of love engenders jealousy, inseparable from passion which itself is a manifestation of human weakness that mocks the fragile constructs of reason and constantly humiliates it. To escape the scrutiny of an ever suspecting *other* (metaphorically, the courtier), the passionate soul weaves a skein of lies and deceit only to learn that passion, which had announced itself as an enduring present of overflowing content, is by nature desiccating and finite. Love promises to exchange time for eternity, but finally gives only inconstancy or flux. Marriage passes for union and is only an arrangement that assures one of a rank in the world. And the counterpulsations of love and politics—inconceivable to us—breeds in the idle court the thousand petty rivalries that suffocate feeling, feeling that survives only as an artificial code of polite gallantry to which men and women alike cynically (and gleefully) subscribe. The Princesse de Montpensier, the Comtesse de Tende, and the Princesse de Clèves all die young, and their final image of death is nothing less than that perspective on emptiness to which their creator was witness. As Pascal wrote, "The last act is always bloody, however fine the rest of the play may be; in the end, they throw some earth over your head, and it is forever finished."

Ménage probably urged the Countess to write and directed her to memoirs and histories of the sixteenth century in which she placed the action of her novel. He may have helped her to write it as well, for she refers to "our Princess" in her letters. Before the *Princesse de Montpensier* could be properly published—anonymously, of course!—a servant purloined one of the manuscript copies and the work began to circulate from hand to hand. "Happily," she wrote to Ménage, "it is not under my name. I beg you, if you hear of it, to act as if you had never seen it, and to deny that it comes from me if by any chance this were said" (C I, 169).

This was not merely refined vanity; she had some excellent reasons to preserve her anonymity. Mademoiselle (the Duchesse de Montpensier) might take umbrage at a work which, however plainly fictitious (as a carefully worded preface made abundantly clear), presented her ancestors in an unflattering and scandalous light. Worse, Madame, like so many other readers who were accustomed by tradition to read all novels as *romans à clef*, might see it for the transposition that it was! Indeed, some readers, including Sorel,[14] did, but not Madame, who apparently read it without tumbling to a thing. In an ironic retransposition where life imitated an art that had itself imitated life, she laughingly said that she would allow Louis XIV to play the character of Chabanes (HHA, 71). Finally, it was considered unfitting for ladies to author books, and Mme de Lafayette was well on her way to becoming a great lady. Huet, who had imprudently revealed the author's identity to his sister, was roundly scolded: "I did indeed give you a *Princesse de Montpensier* for Araminte, but not to give as one of my works. She will think that I am a real professional author, to be giving my books around like that. Please try to repair what this might have spoiled in the opinion that I want her to have of me" (C I, 175).

IV *La Rochefoucauld*

Just the year before *La Princesse de Montpensier*, Somaize's *Grand Dictionnaire des précieuses* had appeared. Mme de Lafayette was never a *précieuse* of the Moliéresque variety, but she was nonetheless listed under the pseudonym of "Féliciane" in this directory of elegant ladies. It was a sign of her rising social standing. She was quoted as explaining, in a rather mannered pose, that the neglectfulness that people reproached her for was not due to ingratitude, but to "idle forgetfulness" (*oubli paresseux*).[15]

For the next few years she led a peaceful existence. She made friends with the Du Plessis-Guénégauds and became a familiar of their sumptuous Hôtel de Nevers (they also possessed a country estate at Fresnes which had been reconstructed by Mansart), a center of literary, social, and political life, and a foyer of the Jansenist doctrine to which her stepfather, Renaud-Réné, had been converted in his declining years. There she met the delightful Pomponne, a secretary of state, and Corbinelli, the secretary of Bussy-Rabutin (Mme de Sévigné's cousin). He too was in Somaize's *Dictionnaire*, as "Corbulon." Mme Du Plessis-Guénégaud had played an important part in the diffusion of Pascal's *Lettres Provinciales*, and she also dabbled in politics. She already hated Mazarin and Colbert and now bore them even more animosity because of her family's involvement in Fouquet's disgrace. Mme de Lafayette probably kept her distance in this matter; acquaintance with Fouquet had caused her a difficult moment before.

At the Hôtel de Nevers she also saw the Duc de La Rochefoucauld, whom she had met earlier, and who had sent his compli-

ments at the time of her marriage (C I, 74). During a tempes-
tuous youth—the "fever of reason," he called it—he had
dreamed of saving France from Richelieu and had witnessed
or participated in the conspiracies of Gaston d'Orléans and
Mme de Chevreuse. He had even proposed to abduct Queen
Anne to rescue her from the Cardinal, but instead ended in the
Bastille. Always on the edge of disgrace, he joined the *Cabale
des Importants* and became an intimate of the great and royal
Condé family. He loved their sister, Mme de Longueville, a
princess of the blood, and had an illegitimate son by her, the
Comte de Saint-Paul. He had taken an active role in the intrigues and battles of the Fronde (at one point attempting to
murder the Cardinal de Retz), and known the treasons, crimes,
and ingratitudes to which self-interest drove his fellow men.
Horribly wounded at the Faubourg Saint-Antoine, one of the
last battles of the civil war, he was half-blind when Mme de
Lafayette saw him at the Hôtel de Nevers. She perhaps remembered bits of his self-portrait that had been published in
Mademoiselle's *Divers Portraits*:

There is something sad and proud in my air; this makes most
people think that I am contemptuous, though I am not at all . . . .
I have wit . . . but it is a wit impaired by melancholy. . . . In general I like reading; best of all I like reading where one can find
something to fashion the mind and fortify the soul. Above all, I take
great satisfaction in reading with an intelligent person, for in this
way one reflects constantly on what one reads, and from the reflections that one makes arises the most pleasant and useful conversation possible. I judge fairly well prose and verse that is shown to
me; but perhaps I state my opinion of it a little too freely. . . . I
was somewhat of a gallant in the past, but no more, however young
I may be [he was forty-six]. I have given up flirtation and am only
surprised that so many respectable people indulge in it. I highly
approve of fine passions; they show greatness of soul, and although
in the worries they cause there is something contrary to hard reason,
they are so well reconciled with the most austere virtue that I think
they cannot be justly condemned. I who know all the delicacy and
strength that there is in the great emotions of love, if ever I come to
love, it will assuredly be in this way; but being the way I am, I do
not think that my knowledge of love will ever pass from my mind
to my heart.

What feminine heart could be insensitive to such a picture?

Melancholy in his disillusion, brooding in his uprightness, this disenchanted prince from one of France's great families, wounded in body and soul, virtually pleaded for a great heart to share and soften his loneliness. Could Mme de Lafayette have remained insensitive? Together she and La Rochefoucauld wrote letters of commiseration to Pomponne, exiled for his involvement with Fouquet. But the Duke soon ceased frequenting the Du Plessis-Guénégauds, perhaps because they were too openly committed to Fouquet (M II, 45–46). He spent all his time at the fastidious Mme de Sablé's, where the good cooking and turning of misanthropic maxims appealed to him.

Mme de Lafayette lost sight of him for a time. She was busy with the publication of *La Princesse de Montpensier* and especially her husband's lawsuits, which had reached a critical stage. In 1662 the Chambre de Conseil, in a most unfavorable decision, ordered Espinasse, Hautefeuille, and Nades sold to satisfy the Lafayette creditors. Ruin was imminent; appeals were immediately filed, delaying tactics adopted, and the enemy sounded out on what terms it might settle for. Meanwhile influence was brought to bear, and a new court decision gave M. de Lafayette full and unencumbered title to Hautefeuille and its revenues. Lafayette could offer the creditors (by now into their third generation) some remuneration, and they decided to settle for half of what was owed them. By the end of 1662, after twenty-odd years in the courts, all the Count's lands and revenues were delivered to him free of lien, and the Lafayettes, at long last triumphant, were complete masters of their domains.

After the successful termination of his lawsuits, M. de Lafayette again returned to Auvergne, and Mme de Lafayette entered a period of idleness, if not boredom. She leafed through Guez de Balzac, but admitted to Huet that she had only slight interest in eloquence (C I, 200). Ménage was at work on a paean to the late Cardinal Mazarin and hardly ever came any more. Huet was in Caen, and Segrais was sharing Mademoiselle's exile at Saint-Fargeau. She tried her hand at writing another novel, but was unsatisfied with it: it was not even worth having Ménage rewrite it (C I, 191). There was Corbinelli, though, fascinating and enigmatic.

Mme de Lafayette and Corbinelli, with Mme de Sévigné, went to Livry one day. While strolling in the gardens, they came to talk of love. Corbinelli and Mme de Lafayette had contrary opinions and decided then and there to write them down. They sat at a nearby rustic table, he at one end and she at the other. Mme de Lafayette composed what she called an "Argument Against Love" (C I, 193).[16] Corbinelli later showed a copy to Mlle de Méry (Mme de Sévigné's cousin), who sent a copy to Huet. Mme de Lafayette was greatly irritated; she had not intended this impromptu effort to be passed around. What would people think of her? However, she did not break with Corbinelli, who happened to be privy to some very interesting secrets. He had become the depository of Guiche's highly compromising letters to Madame and was seeking to return them to Madame, perhaps through Mme de Lafayette and her sister-in-law, Mère Angélique of the Chaillot convent (M II, 77). Hoping to endear himself to Madame, Vardes took a hand in the proceedings, and Mme de Lafayette withdrew to a prudent distance. Her husband arrived for a stay of three months, and then again there was nothing to do. In August 1663 she wrote to Ménage: "I am all alone in Paris. Seriously, I don't see anybody here and I spend whole days indoors without being interrupted by any visitors" (C I, 199).

At the end of September she decided to join Madame at Villers-Cotterets. The Princess had just broken with Guiche, who was on his way to the Polish armies, but she did not lack for gallants. Vardes was present, and so was the Prince de Marcillac, eldest son of M. de La Rochefoucauld. *Tiens*! The Duke's memoirs had appeared at the end of 1662, and Mme de Lafayette probably began to read them—with great interest. She also returned to the Hôtel de Nevers to commiserate with Mme Du Plessis: her husband and her brother had at last been clapped in the Bastille. Of course M. de La Rochefoucauld also came to offer sympathy, and thus there was a chance to see him when he was not closeted with Mme de Sablé. How to draw him away from Mme de Sablé?

In her youth, Mme de Sablé had been one of the stars of the Hôtel de Rambouillet. In her own salon she received Mme de Longueville, the Duc d'Enghien, and other *seigneurs* whose conversation was so unrestrained that Mazarin, whiffing an odor of sedition, had the house watched. Unhappy in marriage, she loved Montmorency, but he had died on the scaffold. Her house was hard to penetrate. She was a hypochondriac who trembled in dread fear of infection or disease, especially those an outside visitor might bring. The porter at her door was particularly warned against admitting any callers who did not seem in good health. She had become a Jansenist and, to avoid contact with co-sectarians who might not be as fastidious as she, a passage from the second story of her house connecting with the Paris convent of Port-Royal and abutting on a small tribune permitted her to worship without fear of infection. The complete *malade imaginaire,* Mme de Sablé dabbled in pharmaceutics, chiefly to concoct the various remedies she was constantly essaying. For La Rochefoucauld, the chief attraction of her house, besides her soups and marmalades, was the visits of the Comte de Saint-Paul, his son by Mme de Longueville. For La Rochefoucauld these meetings were demanding exercises in restrained emotion, for the young Count was ignorant of his true paternity.

How was Mme de Lafayette to force her way into this cenacle? Emile Magne suggests she may have rashly asked Mme de Sablé for a medicine or remedy of hers, which was sure to convince the Marquise that she was unfit to be admitted (M II, 91). Moreover, Mme de Lafayette's general health was known to be poor. Whatever the reason, she was not invited to join the company, and was quite put out: ". . . I am very offended and this makes me realize that I am more devoted to you than I thought, for there are certainly few people in the world who could offend me by not wishing to see me any more" (C II, 17). Mme de Lafayette persisted nonetheless, keeping the Marquise informed of Madame, consoling her for the loss of a friend (C I, 192); finally the ban was lifted in her favor. She cannot have been the confidante of all their activities and was certainly ignorant of their literary endeavors. When La Rochefoucauld's *Maximes* appeared in 1664, she was completely shocked. Arriving from Fresnes where she had spent a few lonely days with Mme Du Plessis, she wrote to Mme de Sablé: "we have read M. de La Rochefoucauld's maxims. Ah, Madame, what corruption one must have in heart and mind to be able to imagine all that!" (C I, 219). She could barely convince herself that the maxims were seriously meant. Mme de Longueville was equally astounded and, worried that her son, destined for the Church, should be exposed to such misanthropic shafts, she forbade him to call at Mme de Sablé's.

However "corrupt" Mme de Lafayette may have thought the

mind and heart of La Rochefoucauld, she was decidedly fascinated by this man. She may even have fallen in love with him, for it is clear that she deliberately seized the opportunity of drawing the Comte de Saint-Paul to her house, knowing that La Rochefoucauld would follow. And this at some embarrassment to herself: the sixteen-year-old Count had heard rumors about her interest in M. de La Rochefoucauld. In an awkward letter to Mme de Sablé, she implored her difficult friend to persuade the boy that it was only a question of friendship: "I thoroughly detest that persons of his age should think that I have gallantries. . . . And moreover, he is more disposed to believe what he is told about M. de La Rochefoucauld than another. Anyway, I don't want him to think anything, except that he is one of my friends, and I beg you to get this out of his head . . . (C II, 10–11).

There were to be rumors of this sort for years to come. Rhymsters hummed of

> La Prude Lafayette
> Et son La Rochefoucauld (M II, 116).

As late as 1675, Mlle de Scudéry wrote Bussy-Rabutin: "M. de La Rochefoucauld lives quite respectably with Mme de Lafayette; nothing shows but friendship. Fear of God on both sides, perhaps policy too, have clipped the wings of love. She is his favorite, his first friend. Nothing could be happier for her or more respectable for him" (M II, 116). Bussy naturally thought he knew better: "Even if at present one sees nothing but respectable relations between M. de La Rochefoucauld and Mme de Lafayette, that doesn't mean that there is only friendship. I maintain that there is still love, and even if it were possible that it had disappeared, there is still something that religion condemns as much as love itself" (M II, 116). In 1677, the *romaniste* again wrote to Bussy: "(M. de La Rochefoucauld and Mme de Lafayette have done a novel on the gallantries of Henri II's court that is said to be admirably well-written; they are not of an age to do anything else together" (Ashton, *Madame de La Fayette*, 103).

Bussy has put the question obliquely, but it is one we continue to ask today: did they sin together? As we have seen, their contemporaries were unsure and puzzled; after all, in 1665 Mme de Lafayette was only thirty-one, and La Rochefoucauld was fifty-two. And gouty and invalid as he was, he mustered enough strength for yet another of the campaigns against the Spaniard in 1667. There is really nothing we can conclude in the absence of any documents other than the gossip quoted above. At best we could say that it was an *amitié amoureuse,* or a sympathy in the deepest sense of the word. All Mme de Lafayette's modern biographers—Magne, Beaunier, Ashton, Pingaud—point out the poor health of the couple, their disabused opinions of precisely this sort of human folly, and believe that this relationship, one of the most fascinating in literary history, was probably a chaste one.[17]

For the first few years, however, until 1668, their friendship was not the indestructible union that it later became. They did return together to the Hôtel de Nevers (where La Rochefoucauld annoyingly admired the fetching Mlle de Sévigné) to greet Pomponne, newly pardoned and promoted to the Swedish ambassadorship. There they heard Boileau recite his satires and Racine declaim three acts of his *Alexandre.* But the Duke was busy. He was at work on a new edition of the *Maximes,* and his son's attentions to Madame had won him Monsieur's easily earned jealousy and an order to return to his province. In 1667, as we have mentioned, he was off to the wars, a last chivalric compulsion, perhaps, or an attempt to curry favor with Louis XIV (M II, 129). And upon his return, he again saw Mme de Sablé, who had previously closed her door to him.

Meanwhile, Mme de Lafayette began her labors as chronicler of the loves of Madame and probably initiated her famous correspondence with Jeanne-Marie-Baptiste de Savoie-Nemours (later "Madame Royale"), whom she had known at Chaillot, and who had just been married to Charles-Emmanuel III, Duc de Savoie (M II, 125). Faithful Ménage, useful for the newsletters he sent M. de Lafayette and sometimes importunate for the embarrassing Latin poems he composed for her, at last committed some bit of foolishness that strained the patience of his "Philis." She wrote him a sharp letter that caused a break of some twenty years in their letters. Because of this and other lacunae in her correspondence, we know little of what she did from 1666 to 1668. She must certainly have been vexed at La Rochefoucauld's return to Mme de Sablé, and perhaps she understood that to win him back, she would have to exploit the intellectual man.

She sent him a manuscript of *La Princesse de Montpensier* (M II, 138), and with Segrais formed the project of writing a novel treating the high deeds of love and knighthood among Christians and Moors in a conventionalized medieval Spain. This did interest La Rochefoucauld, and the trio set to work with a will. They must have been vastly amused and delighted in concocting the shipwrecks and rescues, dalliances, infidelities and battles, the *questions d'amour,* and the whole metaphysics of love that fill the pages of *Zaïde.* Mme de Lafayette's hand may be discerned in the treatment of love and its psychopathic derivative, jealousy. Segrais, who vaunted his experience in the "rules of art," took charge of the plot and its outlines. He also did the necessary historical documentation. Mme de Lafayette drew the psychology of the characters, and La Rochefoucauld criticized, rewrote, and polished the hesitant style of his friend.[18] (Mme de Lafayette was not a "natural" writer.) Huet was also associated with the common effort. Mme de Lafayette wrote to him: "I am sending you the third and fourth notebooks [of *Zaïde*]. The latter one has not been gone over or corrected at all, so you will find plenty to 'bite on'; but don't spend time on the expressions, just look at the action, for when we have corrected it, you'll go over it again. . . . Use red pencil, we can't see the black" (C II, 22–23). The learned Huet also contributed a weighty introductory essay called "On the Origin of Novels."

The famous publisher Claude Barbin put the first volume on sale at his establishment by the Sainte Chapelle. It was an immediate success, and the second volume followed in 1671.[19] Author (with some help) of two successful novels, Mme de Lafayette felt sure enough of her style and sense of language now to circulate two little writings in which she satirized certain mannered ways of speaking: the first was known as the "Lettre du Jaloux,"[20] purportedly written by a jealous *précieux* lover to his mistress; the second, "Sur les mots à la mode," ridicules the affected and meaningless turns of speech of the *petits marquis.*[21] With certain exceptions, Mme de Lafayette always eschewed period clichés and figurative expressions, and in this little parody, she turns in derision the cascades of synonymous expressions and complementary paraphrases so opposed to her own style of writing.

V   O nuit désastreuse! O nuit effroyable:

The Death of Madame

In 1669, Madame remembered her ambition to have her friend write her memoirs, and most of September and October were so spent, completing the Princess' adventures up to the time of Guiche's departure for Poland. In June of 1670, Madame returned from a diplomatic mission in England. She had assured her brother's support for Louis XIV's war against Holland and had reason to feel triumphant, for she was, as Mme de Lafayette wrote, "at twenty-six years of age the link between the two greatest kings of this century" (HHA, 79). But she was unhappy because of her insufferable husband, who not only made her life wretched with his jealousies, but also had inflicted no less than eight pregnancies upon her, six of them resulting in miscarriages. Mme de Lafayette drove to see her at Saint-Cloud, arriving at ten at night. She found Madame walking in the gardens, feeling rather ill with a pain in her side. This was Saturday, June 28. On Sunday Madame heard mass and watched her daughter being painted by an artist, perhaps Peter Lely (HHA, 218, n. 3).

Lying down on some cushions near Mme de Lafayette, Madame went to sleep. "During her slumber she changed so considerably that after having watched her for some time I was surprised, and I reflected that her vivacity must have contributed greatly to adorn her face, since it made her so lovely when she was awake, and so little when she was asleep."[22] When she awakened, she began to chat with a newly arrived guest and drank a chicory infusion (popular as an iced drink). Almost immediately she cried out "Oh! what a pain in my side! Oh, the pain! I can't bear it!" Her ladies rushed her to bed. "I was supporting her while they were unlacing her. She was still moaning, and I saw that she had tears in her eyes. I was astonished and moved, for I knew her to be the most patient person on earth. Kissing the arms that I held, I said to her that she must be in great suffering; she replied that it was unbearable." Doctors were called; Madame cried out that she was going to die, and asked for a confessor.

"Monsieur was by her bed; she embraced him and said, with a sweetness and countenance capable of moving the most bar-

barous of hearts: 'Alas! Monsieur, you stopped loving me long
ago; but that is unjust: I was never unfaithful to you.' Monsieur seemed very touched and so was everyone in the room, so
that the only noise heard was the sobs of weeping people."

Suddenly Madame asked someone to look at the drink she had
just swallowed; she believed that it had been poisoned and
called for an antidote. Mme de Lafayette was standing near
Monsieur, and although she believed him incapable of such a
crime, she nevertheless observed him fixedly, "out of an astonishment common to human malignity." He seemed "neither
upset nor embarrassed by Madame's opinion. He ordered that
some of the infusion be given to a dog, and agreed with
Madame that oil and counter-poison be brought in order to
dissuade Madame of such a dreadful thought."

The chamber lady who had prepared the infusion drank
some of it herself, and emetics were ineffectively administered
to Madame. They only served to convulse her horribly, and she
cried that the pain was undiminished.

It seemed that she was entirely certain of her death and that she
accepted it like an indifferent thing. . . . Monsieur called Mme de
Gamaches to feel her pulse; the doctors had not thought of it. She
left the bed in a fright, saying that she could feel none, and that all
Madame's extremities were cold. This frightened us, and Monsieur
was scared. M. Esprit [Monsieur's doctor] said these were ordinary
symptoms of a colic and that he vouched for Madame's life. Monsieur
became furious and replied that he had vouched for M. de Valois
[Monsieur and Madame's infant son], and that he had died; that
he vouched for Madame, and that she was dying too.

Two more royal doctors arrived and assured Monsieur upon
their lives of Madame's safety. Instead of the emetic that she
asked for, they prescribed a purge and bleeding. Madame maintained that there was no remedy to her illness, "but she said this
with the same composure and sweetness as if she had spoken of
an indifferent thing." When her ladies whispered that she
seemed better, Madame overheard and cried out: "There is so
little truth in that, that were I not a Christian I would kill myself, the pain is so unbearable. One must not wish ill to any person," she added, "but I wish someone could feel for a moment
what I am suffering, to know what it is like."

The doctors became worried, and when the King arrived

about eleven Sunday night, they reversed themselves, said the case was hopeless, and urged administration of the last rites. Bossuet was sent for. Louis XIV approached Madame, wept, and bid her adieu. M. Feuillet heard her general confession and then Montague, the English ambassador, arrived. Mme de Lafayette, following their conversation in English, heard Madame urge the ambassador not to speak of poison to her brother, nor to seek vengeance against the French king. She received the last sacrament, and the doctors came again to bleed her; but no blood came. M. de Condom (Bossuet) arrived and hurried to her side to direct her last thoughts to God. As he was speaking, Madame's first chamber lady came near, and Madame told her in English, so that Bossuet would not understand, "When I am dead, give M. de Condom the emerald ring that I had made for him." She kissed the crucifix that the bishop gave her and fell back on her bed. "Her agony lasted only a moment; after two or three convulsive movements of her lips, she expired at two-thirty in the morning, nine hours after she was taken ill."

Madame's death profoundly affected Mme de Lafayette. It was like a symbolic tragedy in which fiction assumed a terrible immediacy: the abstract intuitions of *La Princesse de Montpensier,* sensed intellectually, had matched the contours of life in the death of this heart that Mme de Lafayette loved. Madame's death served to confirm her prejudicial views; she sensed that her illogical association of love and unhappiness had been borne out in experience. The promises of Madame's life had been illusory; for Madame, it would indeed have been "enough to be." In this refraction of life, fixed by her lucid observation, we see the link between Mme de Lafayette the witness and memorialist, and Mme de Lafayette the analyst and novelist of self-destructive passion. Madame's resignation and calm were an example of restraint that she faithfully imitated in the style of her relation: her language is outwardly sober and impersonal, but by the gestures and words she describes, it clearly conveys the feeling of an awesome, because meaningless, finality. And this is done without the terse harshness that sometimes characterizes the style of *La Princesse de Montpensier.* It is sentiment without sentimentalism, close to what Gide meant when he defined Classical style as an art of implication and understatement, as "l'art de dire le plus en disant le moins." Somewhere in the distance separating her "divine reason" from the "disorders of love" was born her particular genius.

VI *Paris and the Publication of*
La Princesse de Clèves

Although Madame's death greatly reduced Mme de Lafayette's access to court, she continued to gather about her people of standing whose good conversation and gossip made her "Saturdays" famous. To them came princes and poets, and of course M. de La Rochefoucauld, a permanent fixture of the house on the Rue de Vaugirard. Segrais, Huet, Corbinelli, the academician Jacques Esprit were habitués, as was Mme de Sévigné, in spite of the fact that her daughter, Mme de Grignan, had little love for the mother's girlhood friend. Even the Cardinal de Retz found himself there, face to face with his old antagonists of the Fronde, La Rochefoucauld and the Prince de Condé. In the reception rooms of the *hôtel* the guests discussed politics and literature and traded gossip. In the summer they moved to their hostess' garden with its little fountain and boxed orange and oleander trees. Mme de Sévigné called it "the prettiest little place in Paris to breathe in" (IV, 542; III, 92). She brought news of her adored daughter and worried about son Charles, who was under the spell of the infamous Ninon de Lenclos. La Rochefoucauld quipped that "Sévigné's ambition is to die of a love that he doesn't have" (C II, 39). The company made fun of the ridiculous Mme de Marans, guilty of having spread rumors about Mme de Grignan's untoward affection for her brother-in-law and, sweetest of all diversions, listened to Segrais' daily reading of passages from *L'Astrée.*

One day Mme de Lafayette and La Rochefoucauld received a visit from the singular Abbé de Choisy, who, along with Monsieur, had a furious penchant for transvestitism. Seeing him arrive in carrings and beauty patches, Mme de Lafayette banteringly confided that such was not the fashion for men and that the Abbé would do better to dress completely as a woman. He took her at her word and returned later to strut in his finest gown, rings, a diamond cross, and "ten or twelve beauty patches." "Ah, the lovely creature!" exclaimed Mme de Lafayette, "you took my advice, and how right you were; just ask M. de La

Rochefoucauld." And the pair turned him round and round in mock admiration.[23]

Mme de Lafayette read Montaigne's *Essays* ("he would have made the most pleasant of neighbors") and defended Pascal's *Pensées* against Nicole's reservations. That austere gentleman took the trouble to rebut her (M II, 179, n. 1). La Fontaine's tales and fables won him an invitation. He honored La Rochefoucauld with "Les Lapins." This fable contains some verses that could apply equally to the works of La Rochefoucauld and Mme de Lafayette:

> Mais les ouvrages les plus courts
> Sont toujours les meilleurs. En cela, j'ai pour guide
> Tous les maîtres de l'art, et tiens qu'il faut laisser
> Dans les plus beaux sujets quelque chose à penser.

La Fontaine made Mme de Lafayette the curious gift of a billiard table. After all, the Countess was known to gamble and even to play cards. With bonhomie he included a small poem in which he compared the new game to the game of love: "The 'pocket' is a proud heart, the ball is a poor lover . . ." (M II, 181–82). If she found La Fontaine amusing, Mme de Lafayette appears to have cared less for his friends Molière and Racine, who were never called to read anything. She found Boileau too witty for his own good: "He who puts himself above others, whatever wit he may possess, puts himself below his own wit."[24] And she probably disliked what he had written about Mlle de Scudéry.

On the other hand, she seems to have liked music, especially Lully's, and she liked painting a great deal. Mignard acquired the habit of exhibiting his paintings at the Rue de Vaugirard and upon occasion sought her advice on his sketches. Her taste for Mignard was shared by Mme de Coulanges, whose husband was Mme de Sévigné's cousin. Apart from letters and *beaux-arts*, Mme de Lafayette's group also enjoyed the pleasures of the table and was offered sumptuous feasts by Gourville, La Rochefoucauld's former valet, a curious and enterprising figure who had become the *homme de confiance* of many great personages, and consequently made his fortune. At one of these dinners she heard Boileau read his *Art Poétique*, which did not give any precepts for the novel. Indeed, it did not mention the novel at all. At the same dinner she met Guilleragues, the anonymous author of one of the great "bestsellers" of seventeenth-century France, the *Lettres Portugaises*.[25] And through the Coulanges she met Mme Scarron, granddaughter of the very protestant Agrippa d'Aubigné, widow of the famous comic writer, future mistress and wife of Louis XIV as Mme de Maintenon.

Mme de Lafayette was not remiss, nor were any of her friends, in maintaining good relations at court. She still went to the Palais-Royal, where Monsieur one day showered her with attentions, "right in the nose of the Maréchale de Clérembault" (who had won the post of governess of Monsieur's daughters over her; C II, 34). The Coulanges were connected with Louvois, the minister of war, whose influence Mme de Lafayette sought in furthering her son's military career. Mme Scarron was governess of the royal bastards and through her Mme de Lafayette met the king's mistress, Mme de Montespan, who made her gifts of writing tables and crucifixes (Sévigné III, 273, 316). Pomponne had become a secretary of state for foreign affairs, and the Prince de Marcillac was one of the king's favorites. Mme de Thianges, sister of *la Montespan,* seized the occasion, in 1674, of her bastard nephew's birthday to spread the fame of the little clan. She had an artisan execute a small gilded chamber, somewhat like a doll's house, furnished with bed and chairs and tiny wax figurines. The little prince, seated in an armchair, was shown handing a poem to La Rochefoucauld, while Mme Scarron looked on. Behind them Bossuet was chatting with the Prince de Marcillac, and in an alcove Mme de Lafayette and Mme de Thianges were reading poems together. Outside a little balustrade was Boileau, flanked by Racine, signaling La Fontaine to approach, and fending off a band of poetasters with a pitchfork. The inscription read *Chambre du Sublime.*

The courtisans took note of the stir this striking gift precipitated and the attention it drew to the illustrious group. Mme de Lafayette was once again invited to the fêtes and illuminations of Versailles. The king granted her elder son, the Abbé Louis de Lafayette, some important ecclesiastical benefices. One day, the monarch honored her with a tour of the palace grounds in his carriage (Sévigné III, 188–89). She seems not to have suffered at all from her connections with the old Frondeurs, who were still suspect to Louis XIV. (And Renaud-René de Sévigné, although nearly dead, was still more suspect, being a Jansenist as well.) Eventually the king gave her a pension of 500 *écus*.

Meanwhile, creative literary activity had not ceased. On December 18, 1671, Barbin, the publisher of *Zaïde*, obtained a *privilège* (royal license and copyright) for several books, among which was a "Prince de Clèves." This seems to have been the tentative title of the novel that has assured Mme de Lafayette's literary fame.[26] It also seems to indicate that originally the novel was to have been another collective undertaking, perhaps intended to distract La Rochefoucauld. The Duke had become increasingly morose; Mme de Sévigné had so sad a conversation with him one day that she wrote her daughter that there seemed to be nothing left but to get buried (III, 92). He suffered terribly from gout, calling upon death to deliver him, and from the chronic affliction of the nobles, boredom. Perhaps he sought release from the latter in raising his white mice and taking part in the elaboration of *La Princesse de Clèves*. The next mention we have of the novel under this title is a letter of March 16, 1672, of questionable authenticity, from Mme de Sévigné to Mme de Grignan: "I am mortified that you received *Bajazet* from someone other than me. It's that damned Barbin, who hates me because I don't write any *Princesses de Clèves* and *Montpensier*" (II, 534–35).[27]

The new book, like *La Princesse de Montpensier*, was set in the sixteenth century and entailed a large amount of historical research. Segrais was again helpful, bringing Brantôme and Castelnau's memoirs to the attention of the author(s). But progress was slow. La Rochefoucauld's mother had died in 1672, and on June 17 of the same year he suffered a terrible blow: he received news that his eldest son, the Prince de Marcillac, had been severely wounded, and that the Duc de Longueville (formerly the Comte de Saint-Paul) and the Chevalier de Marcillac (his fourth son) had been killed outright, all in the same battle, the crossing of the Rhine. La Rochefoucauld did not weep; he said his tears were inside him, flowing in the depths of his heart (Sévigné III, 109). Mme de Lafayette had to nurse him slowly back to moral health. She encouraged him to take up his maxims again in 1673 (Sévigné III, 212, 219) and eventually interested him once more in the documentation of *La Princesse de Clèves*. The readings were extensive: they included histories of some seven reigns of the kings of France from Francis I to Louis XIII by Pierre Mathieu; Mézeray's histories of France; Godefroy's books on court ceremonials; and Father Anselme's genealogies, where Mme de Lafayette found information on the Clèves family.[28]

Work was interrupted by a visit from M. de Lafayette and another lawsuit. In 1675, Mme de La Rochefoucauld died, and in 1676, Renaud-René de Sévigné. The same year Segrais took leave of the Countess; at last he had found a good match in Caen. In spite of the interruptions, Mme de Lafayette pursued her historical readings. The Anne Boleyn episode was taken from Maucroix's 1676 translation of Sanders' *De Origine ac progressu schismatis anglicani*. She may also have read a novel by Mme de Villedieu, *Les Désordres de l'amour*. Like the Princesse de Clèves, the heroine of this mediocre romance admits to her husband that she loves another man, in this case his nephew.

In the same year she received a visit from the Savoyard ambassador, who had come to France to announce the death of Charles-Emmanuel, husband of Mme de Lafayette's friend "Madame Royale." This lady certainly needed influential friends in France, for she had a bad reputation, having made her lover prime minister. Her regency was not likely to stabilize the affairs of the tottering duchy. It is difficult to discern what services Madame Royale asked of her friend, but the latter was soon corresponding regularly with her secretary, Lescheraine. In the beginning Madame Royale seems to have been mainly interested in fashion and news of society, and their relationship, all in all, was rather innocent. Mme de Lafayette was certainly no secret agent. At this juncture that would have been an extremely imprudent line of conduct, for she needed Louvois' favor to establish son Armand in his military career. In 1677, Armand was eighteen, and Louvois obtained a lieutenancy for him and promised a regimental command as soon as a vacancy occurred. Mme de Lafayette had excellent relations with Louvois, whose letters to her are almost obsequious in tone. (In 1679, she arranged a marriage between his daughter and La Rochefoucauld's grandson.)

Finally, after some six or seven years of work, *La Princesse de Clèves* was ready for publication. It was already being read in manuscript form in several *salons*, and we know from letters of Mlle de Scudéry and Bussy that public rumor attributed the work to Mme de Lafayette and La Rochefoucauld.[28] Here we must examine the question of La Rochefoucauld's participation in the writing of the novel. It is an important question for Mme de Lafayette's literary reputation, which is obviously diminished if the novel is the fruit of a collaboration. Most annoyingly, as is the case for other important questions about Mme de Lafayette and La Rochefoucauld, there is no definitive answer, and we are reduced to interpreting secondary evidence. To begin with, Mme de Lafayette's correspondence certainly does nothing to confirm her reputation as a writer. She was a negligent and careless letter writer who all too clearly disliked writing, and said so (C II, 42). (To Ménage she once wrote: "How in heaven's name can you think that my letters are beautiful and eloquent? They can never be so, whatever care you have taken to teach me to write . . ." (C II, 204). If we did not know from other sources that she was possessed of a keen and lively mind, we might be persuaded that the image she so often cultivated in her correspondence, that of an idle and nonchalant woman who merely had a gift for making important friends, was a true one. Thus opinions differ. In the seventeenth century the Abbé Drouyn even made La Rochefoucauld sole author of *La Princesse de Clèves*. Modern scholars are divided. Mr. Ashton gave full credit to Mme de Lafayette, while Emile Magne flatly stated that all her fictional works were the work of a group (M II, 197).[29] More recently, M. Charles Dédéyan, for whom the moral of *La Princesse de Clèves*, "an example of disinterested virtue," is an antidote or reaction to the *Maximes* that had so shocked Mme de Lafayette, sees La Rochefoucauld as a reluctant collaborator whose contributions were more of a formal and stylistic nature.

There is no reason to disbelieve or even discount Mme de Lafayette's indirect admission of authorship, however ambiguous it may seem, in this letter to Ménage in 1691:

You may speak, in your *Histoire de Sablé*, of the two little stories you spoke about yesterday [*La Princesse de Montpensier* and *La Princesse de Clèves*], but I ask you please not to name anyone in either case. I don't believe the persons you mention [Segrais and La Rochefoucauld] had any share in them, except for a little correction.

"It is enough to be"

The persons who are your friends do not admit having any part in this, but what would they not admit to you? (C II, 182)

The "persons" of the last sentence are clearly Mme de Lafayette alone, as reticent about her literary activities as ever, and the circumlocutions are intended to put off the secretary to whom this letter was dictated.

Finally, to convince ourselves that La Rochefoucauld had little to do with the composition of *La Princesse de Clèves,* we have only to compare it, first to *La Princesse de Montpensier,* in which La Rochefoucauld had little part, and then to *Zaïde,* in which he had a considerable part. There is no doubt that in style, structure, and tone, *La Princesse de Clèves* most closely resembles Mme de Lafayette's first novel, and therefore bears a stamp that is unmistakably hers. *Zaïde,* on the other hand, differs from the two other works by its episodic structure and heroic adventures and is more clearly a collaborative production.

Whatever the case may be, these rumors were naturally good prepublication publicity. The confession scene of *La Princesse de Clèves* was already causing a great deal of talk, and someone, perhaps Donneau de Visé or Barbin, evidently thought it good enough to make a short story in itself. Donneau's *Mercure Galant* of January 1678 carried an unsigned short story, "La Vertu malheureuse," that incorporated all the principal elements of Mme de Lafayette's novel: a confession to a husband, an admission of love to a lover, the husband's death, and the heroine's subsequent refusal to marry the lover. The origin of the story remains a mystery.[30]

At last the novel was printed and Barbin put it on sale on March 17, 1678. It was immediately controversial. The *Mercure Galant,* in the first *enquête littéraire* in the history of French letters, asked its readers whether the Princesse de Clèves was right or wrong to tell her husband of her love for the Duc de Nemours. And to begin this sounding of public opinion, it published a highly favorable anonymous letter (attributed to Fontenelle). Most of the *Mercure's* correspondents throught that the Princess was wrong and extravagant. Bussy wrote a letter to Mme de Sévigné condemning the book's shortcomings, and in general, people were "at each other's throats over this book" (C II, 63). By the end of the year Boursault had put on a tragedy based on the novel. As its fame spread, more and more people began to whisper that Mme de Lafayette and La Rochefoucauld were the authors; the first English translation of 1679 alluded to this alleged dual authorship in its subtitle: *The Princess of Clèves.* "The most famed Romance written in French by the greatest Wits of France. Translated into English by a Person of Quality at the request of some friends." As early as April the book's fame had crossed the Alps, and Mme de Lafayette was obliged to deny to Lescheraine that she or La Rochefoucauld had any hand whatsoever in it; she added that she though it a very good book, an excellent imitation of the court and court manners, so that it should really be called memoirs rather than a novel (C II, 63). Thus Mme de Lafayette and her friend adopted a common line: while denying they were the authors of the novel they would praise it to the skies and defend it against criticism. The latter was soon to come.

In December 1678 an anonymous volume, the *Lettres à Madame la marquise de * * * sur le sujet de la Princesse de Clèves,* came into Mme de Lafayette's hands. It was a full-scale criticism in three parts, dealing with technique and composition, the characters' feelings, and the grammar and style of her novel. Rumor attributed the book to the grammarian, Father Bouhours, who vigorously denied authorship. And in fact the *Lettres* were the work of Jean Baptiste Henri du Trousset de Valincour, a friend of Boileau and Racine, later the royal historiographer and Racine's successor in the French Academy. Valincour's intention was "not to oppose the deserved admiration of the public, but to teach it not to admire the faults as well . . ." Many of Valincour's criticisms seemed justified: he deplored the long opening description of the Valois court, the digressions that periodically interrupt the action (although he applauded the Vidame de Chartres episode), the *invraisemblance* of Nemours' presence when the Princess confesses her love for him to her husband. He questioned the introduction of imaginary characters into historical situations. He thought that "Madame de Clèves is an incomprehensible woman: she is the most coquettish prude and the most prudish coquette ever seen" (*Lettres,* 223). Particularly offensive to Mme de Lafayette must have been his allegation that the famous confession scene was taken from *Les Désordres de l'amour.* This is a good example of why Valincour's points are picayunish, for even if we grant that Mme de Lafayette plagiarized Mme de Villedieu, the latter's scene completely lacks the intense psychological agony that *La Princesse de Clèves* generates. Valincour, while not blind to the novel's worth, often founders in moralistic strictures and nitpicking (especially in his grammatical remarks). But his reservations were widely echoed, and Mme de Lafayette's friends and acquaintances—Corbinelli, Bussy, Mme de Sévigné—were equally critical.

The following year Barbin published the *Conversations sur la critique de la Princesse de Clèves.* They were the work of Jean Antoine, Abbé de Charnes. The author's occasional reliance on "inside information" is evidence that Mme de Lafayette was behind this countercritique.[31] The *Conversations* are seldom credited with being an effective rebuttal of Valincour, and it is true that on some issues, notably the weak justification of the digressions as interesting in themselves, Mme de Lafayette's self-defense lacks incisiveness. The refutations are peremptory and ill-humored, and invective substitutes for argument. They nevertheless occasioned some interesting comments on the novel—the "new novel" one is almost tempted to say—with its emphasis on psychological realism and that realism's mediator, history. To the extent that Mme de Lafayette approved and perhaps even dictated Charnes' book, the following quotation shows how closely she approximated that generalized esthetic position that we rightly or wrongly call Classicism:

> The pleasure of fiction consists in perfect imitation. But it is not necessary, as the critic [Valincour] thinks, that the object represented be perfect. Nature that we strive to imitate does not produce that sort. It suffices that objects be depicted such as one has shown the intention to depict them. One is not obligated to make them seem beautiful in everything. One has only to show their beautiful side, remove unpleasant ideas, and show them consonant with nature . . . the great merit is to abandon truth and nature only rarely. *(Conversations,* unpaginated Preface)

This is precisely how Mme de Lafayette used her sources. Brantôme and Castelnau's memoirs abound in licentious and anecdotal stories that she submitted to "truth and nature" (the terms are virtually interchangeable), to reason. And reason, to Mme de Lafayette, does not mean logic, it means *order.* Lengthy physical descriptions are reduced to symbolic notations;

a simple general affirmation suffices, and thus Nemours is simply presented as a *chef-d'œuvre de la nature;* and anything crude or vulgar is suppressed. Through careful pruning and cutting, Mme de Lafayette shaped her sources to her purpose: "It is easy to abridge . . . and only say half of things. The question is to abridge and still express everything" (*Conversations*, 321).

While her use of history is never fanciful, it is clearly an adjunct or prop whose purpose is to lend credibility to her fiction. The kind of story that *La Princesse de Clèves* aspires to be is neither pure fiction (*roman*) nor embroidered history (*histoire galante*), but a third type "in which one invents a subject that is not universally known; one embellishes it with several historical incidents that support its verisimilitude, and arouse the reader's curiosity and attention." We have already seen that Mme de Lafayette described her novel to Lescheraine as "memoirs"; in the *Conversations* it is called an *histoire suivie*, a kind of extension of history through sustained and consistent narrative: "This is not an Epic Poem, nor a Novel, nor a Tragedy. It is an *histoire suivie* that represents things in the way they happen in the normal course of events" (*Conversations*, 136). It is quite clear that *La Princesse de Clèves* was, or wanted to be, something out of the ordinary, and should have been judged accordingly. "It is for the rules to adapt themselves to the taste of a century as refined as ours." If the rules—the literary shibboleth of French Classicism—condemn *La Princesse de Clèves*, then we need new rules (*Conversations*, 145–46).[32] To the moral objections that Valincour raised, the *Conversations* replied: "the author of *La Princesse de Clèves* had no other purpose than to show in a pleasing fictional work that the most innocent gallantries, between married persons, only cause sorrows."

VII   *"A Hundred Arms"*

La Rochefoucauld was slowly dying, as were his friends. Mme de Sablé died in 1678, and Mme de Longueville in 1679. Of old men, La Rochefoucauld wrote: "Each day takes from them a bit of themselves; they no longer have enough life to enjoy what they have, and still less to attain what they desire; before them they see only sorrows, illnesses, and degradation;

everything has been seen, nothing can have for them the charm of novelty" (*Œuvres* I, 346–47). La Rochefoucauld fell seriously ill with fever and a strong depression. On March 15, 1680, he could not receive Mme de Lafayette, and Bossuet administered the last rites of the church. The following day he seemed better, but on the 17th he suddenly died.

"Where will Mme de Lafayette find another such friend?" wrote Mme de Sévigné. "Poor Mme de Lafayette no longer knows what to do with herself; M. de La Rochefoucauld's loss has made such an emptiness in her heart that she better understands the value of such a fine relationship: everyone except her will be consoled . . ." "She is no longer the same person; I don't think her heart will ever lose the feeling of such a loss . . ." (Sévigné VI, 312, 338, 340). Mme de Grignan cynically observed: "One closes ranks, the gap won't be noticed." And this seems to be the conclusion of Mme de Lafayette herself. Late in life she expressed the ultimate truth of such losses by saying: "One does not die of anyone else's death" (C II, 203). However disabused she may have been at that time, in 1680 she was inconsolable and profoundly discouraged. Her fragile health was badly shaken.

Perhaps to distract her mind, she increased her maneuvers on behalf of Madame Royale. Life had to continue, and Mme de Lafayette had a predilection for the political life, even if she was always on the fringes of it. She helped stop publication of a genealogy unflattering to Madame Royale, had libelous pamphlets confiscated, and distributed Savoyard funds to various gazettes (M II, 254). But she was never actually a spy. In fact she was most often totally unaware of the state of political affairs in Savoy and knew nothing of import to communicate concerning France's designs. As Emile Magne puts it, "The Countess was a publicity agent useful for her important acquaintances. Louis XIV, Louvois, and Madame Royale used her in turn for purposes that she did not perhaps suspect at all. Both sides appreciated the contacts that she zealously maintained. Whence her credit in both courts" (M II, 257). This explains to some extent Louvois' patient replies to her incessant letters about her son Armand.[33] In 1680 he had procured a colonelcy for him, and helped him change garrisons. In 1682 Louvois was constrained to inform Mme de Lafayette of her son's irresponsible conduct in Strasbourg. In the company of two other officers, he was accused of having eaten meat on fast days, of insulting passersby, of breaking up a wedding party, of stoning some windows, and of generally scandalizing the *Strasbourgeois.* Mme de Lafayette sent denials of which Louvois apprised the king. Having decided that Armand's principal fault was having fallen into bad company, Louvois arranged for his suspension from active duty to be remanded.

In 1683, M. de Lafayette died, and a gap in Mme de Lafayette's correspondence prevents us from knowing what her feelings were. We do know that she took full charge of the family fortune and administered it to the satisfaction of her sons: "Never has a person, without leaving her place, done such good business. . . . See how Mme de Lafayette is rich in friends on every side and of every rank: she has a hundred arms, she reaches everywhere. Her children appreciate this and thank her daily for having such a winning nature" (Sévigné VII, 315–16).

Sometime during these last years of her life, probably between the death of La Rochefoucauld and 1688, Mme de Lafayette again turned to fiction, this time to write *La Comtesse de Tende,*[34] a novella that was posthumously published in 1724 after it was found in the papers of her elder son. Characteristically, there is no mention of the work in any of her letters, and the dating of the work is based largely upon internal evidence: a Jansenist coloring of sentiment, a firmness of style, an accrued harshness in its treatment of love. As if to prove herself against public opinion by scandalizing it (although *La Comtesse de Tende* remained unpublished during her lifetime), Mme de Lafayette composed another confession scene. But unlike the situation in *La Princesse de Clèves,* where conscience (however suspect its hidden motives) motivates the confession, here an illicit pregnancy is the cause. Shame and ambition, self-interest and jealousy are the emotions that underlie every thought and action of the characters in their blind rush to the abyss. *La Comtesse de Tende* is a harsh, even cruel story, certainly the harshest Mme de Lafayette ever wrote. The heroine dies in abject dishonor. "It costs one dearly to become wise; it costs one's youth" (C II, 192).

For nearly twenty years Mme de Lafayette had not seen Ménage. The poor valetudinarian had recently had a bad fall and was nearly invalid. Mme de Lafayette, perhaps from a melancholy desire to renew her ties with the vestiges of a vanishing youth, decided to write her old suitor. After inquiring after his health, she closed by saying: "I beg you to believe that all my life I shall be concerned with your well-being, and that my ingratitude toward you is only apparent." And to stimulate her septuagenarian cavalier, she signed with her maiden name, "De La Vergne," and added a coquettish postscript: "Please let me know who wrote the Italian phrase you once told me: *Ardo si, ma non t'amo.* All I know comes from you" (C II, 119–20). Ménage was touched and flattered, knowing that the Countess had done him a singular honor by writing in her own hand: "I have read [your letter] a thousand times, and often covered it with my tears. And I keep it in my favorite box like a precious jewel" (C II, 165–66).[35] Ménage was thus reconquered, and and Mme de Lafayette was careful this time to flatter his vanity, and sincerely, for she prized his friendship: "it is dear to me for its own worth, dear because at present it is my only one. Time and old age have taken away all my friends" (C II, 178). In spite of his infirmities, Ménage was not entirely useless, and so she used him, in a lawsuit of her friend Mme du Tott, and in establishing a genealogy of the Lafayette family.

Mme de Lafayette's letters show her increasing preoccupation with her health, bearing her complaints of pains, rheumatisms, and "vapors." Despite this, her "hundred arms" were not idle, and she was busy arranging a marriage for Armand. She aspired to a match with the Marquis de Lassay's daughter, Marie-Constance-Adélaïde, whose mother had left her a vast fortune. The Countess had gained Lassay's confidence, and when he left to fight the Turks with the Polish king, he gave his power of attorney to Mme de Lafayette. Louis XIV changed his mind about allowing Lassay and his companions to leave. Pretending not to know anything, Lassay hurriedly crossed the border. The king was vexed, but hardly to the extent that Mme de Lafayette gave out to Lassay. Upon his return she urged him to avoid arrest by taking refuge in the provinces. And he received a mysterious *lettre de cachet* forbidding him to dispose of his daughter without royal permission. Mme de Lafayette offered to use her influence with Mme de Maintenon and Louvois, and Lassay gratefully agreed. But then Segrais wrote him, suggesting that his difficulties might vanish if he married his daughter to—Armand de Lafayette. Lassay suddenly realized that he was being maneuvered. He denounced Mme de Lafayette, appealed to Mme de Maintenon, and obtained the annulment of the *lettre de cachet*. Later he married his daughter to the Comte de Coligny (M II, 273–77).

Not to be daunted by this setback, Mme de Lafayette looked for another candidate, and soon found one in Anne-Madeleine de Marillac, descended from an old Auvergnat family. With a dowry of 200,000 *livres,* she was a fine match, and Armand was duly married to her in December 1689. The *Mercure Galant* printed a magnificent wedding notice, and the young couple was presented at court.

As we can see, despite what Mme de Lafayette wrote Ménage about her health and declining powers, she was not inactive. And during these same years she found time to put pen to paper in a purely historical effort. Her years of background reading for *La Princesse de Clèves* and her chronicle of Madame's misadventures must have left her with a taste for historical narration. She set about writing an objective account of public events that was posthumously published in 1731 as *Mémoires de la Cour de France pour les années 1688 & 1689*. She was admirably well placed to write these memoirs, for her house was a veritable information center. For military affairs there was the Prince de Conti (Henri-Jules de Bourbon), Louvois, and of course Armand. For foreign affairs there was M. de Villars, for Spain; the Marquis de La Trousse, for Savoy; the Cardinal d'Estrées, for the Vatican; and the Duc de Lauzun, for England. Mme de Sévigné complained that there was all too much talk of politics for her taste.

The first editor of the *Mémoires* asserted that Mme de Lafayette had long kept such annals and that the Abbé de Lafayette had retained only the fragments for the years in question. Nothing proves this claim is so, but given Mme de Lafayette's singular taciturnity concerning her writings, nothing disproves it either. The *Mémoires* are a rather dry narrative of the political and military events of 1688 and 1689: the War of the League of Augsburg, the English Revolution, the campaign against the Prince of Orange. There are some astonishingly masculine accounts of battles ("The trench was taken by storm and many enemies were killed. It was a fine little action."), often told in the first person plural. There are several sour remarks on the king's newfound piety. Of Mme de Maintenon's

Saint-Cyr, a convent for poor but *honnête* young ladies, she wrote: "this place, which, now that we are devout, is the dwelling place of virtue and piety, might become in a not distant future that of debauchery and impiety . . ." There is also a new sardonic tone, especially where the former Widow Scarron is concerned: "Madame de Maintenon, to entertain her little girls and the king, had a play written by Racine, the best poet of the times, who was taken away from his poetry, in which he was inimitable, to make, for his misfortune and that of those who love the theater, a very imitable historian. She ordered the poet to write a play [*Esther*], but to choose a religious subject; for at the present time, outside of piety there is no salvation at court, as in the other world" (*Mémoires*, 150). We learn that Mme de Lafayette did indeed believe that Madame had been poisoned,[36] that she was scornful of the king's liking for Jesuits, and that she greatly admired Louvois (157, 161). But all in all, with the possible exception of her correspondence, the *Mémoires* are the least memorable of all her writings.

After her son's marriage and the birth of her granddaughter —such a *plaisante demoiselle* that Mme de Lafayette was not even disappointed she was not a boy (C II, 187)—she could be satisfied with her life and accomplishments. Half-seriously, half-mockingly, she wrote to Ménage: "Find another woman [if you can] with a face like mine and interested in the finer things as you taught me, and who has done as much for her family. These things are only rarely joined" (C II, 208). Nevertheless, she began to think of the end. She had never been a religious person (God plays no role in any of her works) and neither were her friends, except for Mme de Sévigné. She sought spiritual advice: "My life is too painful to fear the end. I willingly submit to God's will; He is the almighty, and on every side, one must at last come to Him" (C II, 179). As early as 1686 she felt the first stirrings of an obscure need dictated by her conviction that nothing in this world is solid or worthy of attachment. She began reading the *Instructions* of Saint Dorotheus of Gaza, newly translated by the Abbé de Rancé.

She had known Rancé at the Hôtel de Nevers as a wordly and dissolute priest, the lover of Mme de Montbazon. Upon his mistress' death in 1656, he underwent a spiritual conversion that led him to embrace God as violently as he had the flesh. In 1663 he became a Trappist and eventually instituted in that order, as Voltaire put it, "a frightening reform." Mme de Lafayette decided to ask him the reasons that had decided him to renounce the world. "I will simply tell you that I left it because I did not find what I was seeking. I wanted a repose [37] it was not capable of giving me." Rancé forced himself to submit his mind, to humiliate his reason. He accepted a Pascalian scheme of submission and found faith. He warned Mme de Lafayette: "God must speak to you and tell you what he has not yet told you." But she had doubts; she was too rational to incline her "divine reason," and the Trappists' terrible austerities and mortifications of the flesh seemed to her excessive (C II, 140–46), she who delighted in plump partridges from Segrais' Normandy and *poulardes* from Ménage's Anjou.

Put off by Rancé's austerity, she nevertheless did not seek out some accommodating Jesuit who might have been more indulgent. In 1692 she found Jacques-Joseph Du Guet, a former Oratorian with Jansenist ties, a priest who knew the ways of society and who was full of charm and intelligence. "As a young man," wrote Sainte-Beuve, "Du Guet had tried his hand at romantic novels and had loved *L'Astrée;* he was just the sort of director the author of *La Princesse de Clèves* needed" (*Portraits de Femmes,* Pléiade ed., 1240n). Alas, Du Guet turned out to be more of a rigorist than Rancé. He attacked her moments of revery, the vanity of her reputation, her easy life. He accused her of seeking ready-made prayers and warned that "Truth will judge you, and you are only in the world to follow it and not to judge it." He admonished her that she would have to begin with the sincere desire to see herself as her Judge did, and that this view was "crushing, even for those most forthrightly against dissimulation" (C II, 169–74). Mme de Lafayette began to read the Psalms, but of her spiritual progress we know little more. Her health was rapidly deteriorating; as she wryly wrote Ménage:

First of all, I am a mortal divinity, to an inconceivable degree. I have intestinal obstructions and indescribably wretched vapors. I have no more spirit, mind, or strength. I find the smallest possible things bothersome; a fly seems like an elephant to me. This is my customary state. The past two weeks I have had fever several times and my pulse has not returned to normal. I have an awful head cold and my vapors, which were only periodic, have become chronic . . .

my legs and thighs have suddenly weakened, so that I can barely raise myself with help; and I am astonishingly thin.

Summoning one last gallantry in favor of this phantom of his former "divinity," Ménage (recalling an epigram from the Greek Anthology) replied that her thinness only made her closer to his heart (C II, 183). In 1692 he was dead.

Mme de Lafayette cut herself off from the world and withdrew into a final solitude. She wrote no more letters and received no one. She revised her will and made some last business arrangements, saw Armand promoted to brigadier and Louis off to Rome in search of a bishopric. On May 22, 1693 she fell into a coma, and on the 25th she expired. Two days later she went to her last repose in Saint-Sulpice, the church where she had been baptized and married. Racine wrote Bonrepaus: "Mme de Lafayette . . . died after having suffered in solitude, with an admirable piety, the rigors of her infirmities; she received much succor from the Abbé Du Guet and some of the Gentlemen of Port-Royal. . . ." [38]

CHAPTER 2

Madame de Lafayette and Two Evolutions of Seventeenth-Century Fiction

In this chapter it is not my intent to trace in any detail the complex evolution of French fiction throughout the seventeenth century. Several excellent studies on the subject are already available.[1] My purpose is rather to note briefly changes in the literary temper of the times that will provide a context for Mme de Lafayette's works and to help the reader assess the limits of her originality. I say "limits" in preference to "extent," for it is excessive to claim, as it was once commonplace to do, that she is the creator of the first psychological novel in France. The truth of the matter is that Mme de Lafayette was neither original in form nor content and that she inherited reforms already underway for several years before she began to write.

Insofar as Mme de Lafayette's works are concerned, two evolutions in French literary history are of paramount importance. The first touches all genres and is familiar to any reader who has a passing acquaintance with Racine. I shall discuss it only briefly. The second concerns the changing forms of prose fiction in the seventeenth century.

I Love in Two Temperaments

In the early part of the century the predominant forms of fiction were tragic tales, romances of chivalry, and sentimental novels informed with a *courtois* spirit of ideal love more medieval than modern. Here love springs from a knowledge of the loved one's perfections. For a model of this spiritual phenomenon in the novel, we turn of course to Honoré d'Urfé's *L'Astrée*. The first volume of this famous pastoral novel was published in 1607 and immediately won long-lasting popularity. (We have seen that it remained a favorite of La Rochefoucauld.) In an idealized setting, D'Urfé's shepherds and shepherdesses analyzed their emotions, established hierarchies of sentiment, and generally indulged in a polite casuistry of love—not precluding some barely sublimated eroticism—that was very much to their readers' taste, especially those of the Hôtel de Rambouillet who sought to cultivate a new moral tone in social intercourse. The novel was of course concerned with something more profound the delicate pirouettes of Astrée and Céladon and their interminable adventures; it expressed a particular vision of love that is evidenced in the following passage. Silvandre is sermonizing Hylas, the Don Juan of the pastoral:

Do you know what love means? It means to die in oneself to be reborn in another, it means to esteem oneself only as long as one is pleasing to the loved one, and, in short, it means a will to transform oneself, if possible, wholly into that person.

Thus love in *L'Astrée*, a spiritual phenomenon, is defined by the possibility of becoming another. It is a union of souls effected through knowledge and founded on esteem. The theme of *L'Astrée*, as Gérard Genette has defined it, is "virtue in the service of pleasure." [2]

It is precisely at this point that we see in the works of Mme de Lafayette and her contemporaries a break with the past; not with the immediate past, but with the past of the first part of the century and its ties with Renaissance culture, particularly its neo-Platonism. The concept of love as knowledge of merit—*amour de connaissance*—is at the very antipodes of Mme de de Lafayette's vision, which shares the new generation's outlook (exemplified in Racine and Guilleragues) on love as an involuntary and often uncontrollable passion.

The question of *amour de connaissance* as opposed to *amour d'inclination* was debated in Mme de Sablé's circle, and we find very strong echoes of the debate in *Zaïde*, a novel, incidentally, that formally presents several similarities with *L'Astrée*. Only its concept of love really differs, but that is the whole difference.

To summarize, our change or contrast opposes love founded upon merit and knowledge, and viewed as a stimulus to *gloire* (for *cœur* and *courage* are synonymous in Corneille), to love resulting from involuntary inclination, in disregard of external considerations, and seen as a fundamentally disruptive passion. To simplify even further, we might call the one a cult of the ideal, enthusiastic and self-creative, and the second a humiliating servitude, toxic and self-destructive. Fascinating as the subject may be, it is not my intention to dwell upon the reasons for this shift, with its varied social, religious, and political overtones,[3] but to concentrate on the second evolution in which Mme de Lafayette was more directly involved. It suffices to remember that Mme de Lafayette's generation, no longer imbued with Renaissance spiritualism, restored to the word "passion" its etymological meaning of suffering.

II *From the* roman *to the* nouvelle

The second evolution is essentially a change in fictional form that takes place from about 1656 to 1680, a period that parallels the literary career of Mme de Lafayette, and which transformed the novel of her youth, an episodic and discursive structure of sentimental adventures, into more moderate and sober narrative forms. The emphasis here falls quite markedly upon the new call for *vraisemblance,* or verisimilitude, in the novel, and is accompanied by a movement from prolixity to intensity. Mme de Lafayette's greatest attainment is not in having originated any of the reforms of the double evolution under discussion, but in having married them in fictional form with an excellence of artistic execution not achieved before her. In brief, she wrote better of subjects that others had already treated, and with a profundity of understanding that they lacked.

While Mme de Lafayette was no innovator—before her there were Racine, the novels of Mme de Villedieu, the *Lettres Portugaises*—she did play an important role in the reshaping of the novel's form. The period of her greatest literary activity, 1662–78, coincides with a significant reorientation of French fiction, as well as the period of the supreme literary attainments of her age.

Two Evolutions of Seventeenth-Century Fiction

i. The Heroic Novel

A literature of thwarted passion already existed at the beginning of the century, but its own conventions prevented it from
dealing with the transgressions of desire; it was "desperately
virtuous,"[4] and though this literature constituted a tradition of
sorts, it was insufficiently rich to form a serious antecedent for
Mme de Lafayette's novels. In spite of the extraordinary success
of *L'Astrée*, no vogue for the pastoral novel as a genre developed. An exchange in Corneille's *La Galerie du Palais*, first performed in the year of Mme de Lafayette's birth, has this to say:

> DORIMANT
> Mais on ne parle plus qu'on fasse de romans;
> J'ai vu que notre peuple en étoit idolâtre.
> LE LIBRAIRE
> La mode est à présent des pièces de théâtre.[5]

If we exclude consideration of comic and satirical novels
(often burlesque thrusts at the extravagances of the pastoral,
such as Sorel's *Berger extravagant*), a woman of Mme de Lafayette's generation would have witnessed two decades of unpre-
cedented favor for heroic novels, or novels of gallant adventures. They were works of pure invention, with characters bearing the names of personages taken from ancient history, pur-
porting to relate adventures forgotten or neglected by the historians, and running to ten volumes and more. Such were La
Calprenède's *Cassandre* (1642–45, 10 vols.) and *Cléopâtre*
(1646–58, 12 vols.) and the novels of Mlle de Scudéry.

Madeleine de Scudéry specialized in representing the fashionable society of her day masquerading in a setting of pseudo-
antiquity. Her novels were equally voluminous: *Le Grand Cyrus*
(1649–53) was in ten parts, and *Clélie* (1654–61; we have seen
that Mme de Lafayette read both of them), which contained
the famous *Carte de Tendre*, numbered no less than 7,316
pages. Molière's satire of these novels summarizes them better
than any gloss I might give. The following is taken from scene
iv of *Les Précieuses ridicules*. Magdelon reproves her be-
wildered father:

MAG. Good heavens! If everyone was like you, a novel would soon be finished. What a fine thing it would have been if Cyrus wed Mandane right at first, and if Aronce had married Clélie straight off!

GORGIBUS. What's she talking about?

MAG. Father, there is my cousin who will tell you as well as I that marriage ought never to take place until after other adventures. To be attractive, a lover should know how to utter fine sentiments, to sigh all that is sweet, tender, and passionate, and his suit should be according to form. First of all, he ought to see the person with whom he falls in love at church, on a walk, or at some public ceremony; or be fatally introduced to her by a friend or relative, and leave her pensive and melancholy. For a time he conceals his passion from the object of his love, and yet he pays her several visits, where there never fails to be discussed some question of love that exercises the wits of the assembly. The day for his declaration comes, which ordinarily should take place in some garden walk while the company is at a little distance, and this declaration is promptly followed by anger, which shows in our blushing and which, for a time, banishes the lover from our presence. Then he finds a way to appease us, to accustom us insensibly to the recital of his passion, and to draw from us that avowal which causes so much pain. After that come the adventures: rivals who upset an established inclination, persecutions of fathers, jealousies arising from false appearances, complaints, despair, abductions, and what follows. That's how things are handled with fine manners . . .

GOR. What the devil is all this nonsense?

These authors saw nothing unusual in their productions. La Calprenède thought his novels were unassailable historically, so long as they were not directly contradicted by history itself.[6] And Mlle de Scudéry, as early as 1641, unblushingly prefaced her *Ibrahim* with the assertion that *vraisemblance* was the keystone of the novel. In *Clélie* she enlarged upon this view: "nothing establishes a well-invented story (*fable*) better than these historical foundations that are glimpsed throughout, and which impose the fiction mixed with the truth."[7] But it is hard, she added, to mix them in such a way as to render them indistinguishable one from another.

The heroic and sentimental novel's outstanding contribution in the progress of fiction toward greater *vraisemblance* was its emphasis on historical settings. That these were incongruous transpositions of contemporary life and mores in La Calprenède and Mlle de Scudéry is really beside the point, for history in the seventeenth century was not an evolved discipline with working principles of its own. History was not distinguishable from memoirs or chronicles; it conformed to ancient models (e.g., Livy) and as such was not a type of writing distinct from any other literary undertaking. Nonetheless, it passed for "truth." This confusion, unthinkable to us, was assiduously exploited by novelists, and indicates their desire to achieve some measure of realism.[8] We should remember too that in the seventeenth century the word "imagination," far from being associated with creative or intuitive reality, was the antonym of truth: *"Imaginations"—"Célestes vérités"* is the famous antithesis in *Polyeucte*. And in Pascal, the imagination is one of the chief *puissances trompeuses*. The very concept of literature as an imaginative configuration of life was hardly accepted, and thus novelists, to escape the kind of criticism leveled at *L'Astrée*, sought to anchor their fictions in a pseudo-historical "truth."

From the historians, novelists took fact and used it as a scheme; they embroidered it with their own narrative enlargements and pretended to re-create a past reality or a "truth" whose authenticity was guaranteed "historically"; at least it might be supposed possible. Having eluded the Charybdis of probability by opting for the Scylla of possibility, they then could set about their real business. Contemporary settings were unacceptable because they were so vulnerable to the criterium of *vraisemblance*: it was patently unlikely that such extraordinary goings-on as customarily formed the substance of such novels could have passed unnoticed and unheard of by contemporaries.

Similar problems beset the theater. In choosing a recent event of Turkish history as the subject matter of *Bajazet*, Racine argued that distance in space was roughly the equivalent of temporal (i.e., historical) distance and that he thus had not infringed upon the principle of *major e longinquo reverentia*.[9] As long as some concessions were made to verisimilitude, critical audiences were generally prepared to accept a spurious re-creation of the past even though its spirit and atmosphere were not respected. Had Mme de Lafayette respected all the historical realities of Henri II's court in *La Princesse de Clèves*—and she never had the slightest inclination to portray its grosser aspects —she would have been attacked on moral grounds.

Novelists therefore had to steer a careful course between

bienséance and *vraisemblance,* and as the century progressed, they leaned toward the latter.[10] Thus, when Valincour attacked *La Princesse de Clèves* on historical grounds, it was not because the novel was an unfaithful portrayal of the Valois court (it has always been evident that it was a transposition of Louis XIV's court), but because the heroine was an invented character.[11]

From writers of memoirs, novelists also gleaned some of their techniques. They learned the virtues of chronological narration, thus avoiding the digressive flashbacks necessary if one agreed, as Mlle de Scudéry did, that the duration of the action should be one year's time (obviously the counterpart of the twenty-four-hour rule in the theater).[12] They also learned the value of creating in the reader the illusion that he was hearing a real person relate his own experiences (although they did not generally adopt first-person narration).[13]

By the time Mme de Lafayette began her literary career, the heroic novel had spent its popularity. The eight volumes of Mlle de Scudéry's *Almahide* (1660–63) were the last grand enterprise of this sort.[14] Readers complained of the length of such productions and the monotony of their adventures, which invariably included shipwrecks, corsairs, battles, abductions, and the like. When Charles Sorel published *De la connoissance des bons livres* in 1671, he expressed the feelings of many readers in describing heroic novels as "Spectacles of mummery whose characters have whimsical clothing, steps, and gestures that move one to laugh and little else." (But he cautioned that it was unfashionable not to have read such books, as they formed "a part of the conversation of several good societies.")[15] For its abusive *invraisemblances,* the novel fell into sudden disrepute, and with it, the very term *roman* became pejorative in meaning and connotative of all the unlikely "mummeries" that Sorel deplored. By 1683, Du Plaisir, in his famous *Sentimens,* could note that "Small tales (*histoires*) have entirely destroyed long novels." Du Plaisir insisted that this was not modish caprice, but an advantage "founded on reason" and to be explained by French impatience and the desire to read quickly. The *nouvelle* had freed fiction of the "fatiguing beauty" of novels that begin by the ending and proceed through flashbacks.[16] Authors had begun to turn toward more controlled forms of fiction.

ii. The *nouvelle*

The novel, not discussed in Classical esthetics, had escaped the work of codification that set rules for the writing of a tragedy, for example. The novel had no Scaliger or Castelvetro; it is not even mentioned in Boileau's *Art Poétique*. Consequently it could develop with a freedom denied (in theory, at least) to other genres. It was generally considered as a minor and inferior subgenre, derived from the epic, and sharing the same rules except that it was a prose work.[17] As such it naturally dealt with heroes of high birth (thus Cyrus, Cleopatra, etc.).

When "romanists," in response to criticism, sought to concoct more believable fictions, they found to their satisfaction that with some changes they could continue much as they had in the past. They began to imitate the histories and memoirs that had lately attracted public favor, borrowing some of their techniques, and increasing their emphasis on the analysis of emotion. Antoine Adam notes that in this respect Mlle de Scudéry's *Clélie* was a transitional work. Its fourth part was profoundly different from the others: there were fewer duels and combats, and more *casuistique du sentiment*.[18] In 1661, she published *Célinte*, a fictional work of only one volume. Novels were published that carefully avoided going by the discredited name of *roman*. Instead, a new type of fiction appeared; these were "separate little stories called *nouvelles* or *historiettes* . . . not at all in the style of old novels, and containing only believable adventures."[19]

There was suddenly a proliferation of new subtitles: *nouvelle, nouvelle galante, nouvelle historique, historiette, histoire* (the last nicely ambiguous, as it means both "story" and "history" in French), and some tried to straddle all forms, such as *Cléonice ou le roman galant. Nouvelle par Mme de Villedieu* (1669). The word *nouvelle*, as today, generally designated shorter forms of fiction. Present usage, however vague, almost always means a *short* story (*récit* means a short novel most often in first-person narration), but in the confusion of shifting seventeenth-century trends, *nouvelle* simply meant a believable or *vraisemblable* novel, anything that was not an exercise in the gymnastics of the heroic novel. Boursault, warning his readers that his *Prince de Condé* (1675) dealt "truthfully" (i.e., historically) with war, but not necessarily with love, called his long book a *petit Roman*. Isaac Claude's preface to *Le Comte de Soissons, nouvelle galante* (1699) begins: "Here is a true story [*h istoire;* again the ambiguity] that I give you under the guise of a novel." His *nouvelle,* which is one of the very few to show any influence of *La Princesse de Clèves,*[20] runs to no fewer than 239 closely printed pages.

In Boileau's notion that "what is true is not always believable," and in the realization that from the perspective of the French Classical esthetic the *vraisemblable* could always be opposed to the *invraisemblable* and the true, some authors found license for elucubration. Consider these gleeful sophisms, drawn from the preface of Donneau de Visé's purely fictional *Nouvelles galantes, comiques et tragiques* (1669): "I have no doubt that some unbelievable things will be found in some of my *Nouvelles;* but the reader will please notice that I am not a poet in this work, but an historian. The poet must stick to *vraisemblance,* and correct truth that is not believable. The historian, on the contrary, must write nothing that is not true; and provided that he is sure of telling the truth, he need have no concern for *vraisemblance.*"[21] Donneau must have read Cervantes.

In this muddled state of affairs, readers nevertheless knew what kind of novel they were being offered (regardless of the name it chose to go by), and favored short narratives: "People began to learn what believable incidents were, by little narratives which became fashionable and which were called *nouvelles;* they could be compared to the true stories of some particular experiences of men." [22] For Sorel, the term *nouvelle* was synonymous with *nouveauté;* it should recount "recently happened events, for otherwise there would be no reason to call them *nouvelles* [news];[23] however, this rule is not always observed. The little stories that are published can pass for *nouvelles* even though they do not bear this title. . . ." And long *nouvelles,* he said, are simply taken for short novels (*petits Romans*)[24]

As examples of French *nouvelles,* Sorel mentioned his own *Nouvelles Françoises* of 1623, Segrais' of the same title (1656), Boisrobert's *Nouvelles Héroiques et amoureuses* (1657), and Scarron's *Nouvelles tragi-comiques* (1661). These are of course collections of tales, but as a single *nouvelle* Sorel cites Mme de Lafayette's *La Princesse de Montpensier:* "This book was widely appreciated for its style, which is altogether the tone of fine society." [25] At first glance it seems anachronistic to see *La Princesse de Montpensier* listed with tales that have more in common with Boccaccio and Cervantes than the novel of sentimental analysis from which it derives, but it is not difficult to grasp what Sorel has in mind. Because *La Princesse de Montpensier* passed for a *roman à clef* (the loves of Madame and Guiche), it therefore fit his definition of a *nouvelle,* a story founded upon newly past events. For this reason, Sorel did not make a distinction that we would make, that is between a literature of *nouvelles* linked on the one hand to the bourgeois and realistic novel, and on the other to the aristocratic, historical, and heroic novel. Thus the burlesque "realism" of which Sorel sees examples in Scarron and Boisrobert is of a Spanish mode quite different from Mme de Lafayette's "realism" that voluntarily associates itself with history and memoirs. (Again the reader is reminded that Mme de Lafayette described *La Princesse de Clèves* as "memoirs.") In fact, there was a competitive atmosphere between the two fictional strains; thus Scarron: "if some *nouvelles* were done in French as well-made as some of Miguel de Cervantes, they would be as appreciated as heroic novels." [26]

Sorel could also complain that the new novel, treating passion with *vraisemblance,* was open to charges of immorality. In today's novel, he wrote,

> everywhere there are men who have designs on married women, who importune them with their suit in order to try to corrupt them; if girls are mentioned, they must be brazen and indiscreet, and fit for shameful commerce on behalf of women who will trick them one day. In these novels can be found several married women who are unfaithful to their husbands and are examples of extreme license. From this come only signal deceptions, and it ordinarily ends with poisonings and murders. [27]

This sounds surprisingly like advance criticism, only slightly exaggerated, of Mme de Lafayette's novels. Concern about opinion such as this, rather than some inborn aristocratic reticence, may well have forestalled the publication of *La Comtesse de Tende* in her lifetime. The "new" novel could be viewed by serious-minded men as wreaking the same sort of havoc in public morality that "new" science was in the domain of traditional beliefs. Molière's famous embroilments with the staging of *Tartuffe* were well-known, and novelists avoided religious subjects. Mme de Lafayette was at best indifferent to them, but we should recall the sober conservatism of her age. Only two years before her birth the Church had forced Galileo to recant his findings through the telescope. In France, religious controversy, principally the quarrels between Jansenists and Jesuits, was a serious matter. Religious literature was read by all classes, and the sinister and secret *Compagnie du Saint-Sacrement* kept vigil over public morality. Novelists were always properly circumspect (and all the more so if their books happened to fit Sorel's description) and were careful to underscore quite heavily in their prefaces or elsewhere the high moral purpose of their works. Mme de Lafayette was no exception, even though she did not sign her books. Her moral concerns are explicitly rendered in the closing sentences of three of her novels. "She might have been [the happiest princess in the world] had virtue and prudence directed all her actions"; "Her life, which was rather short, left inimitable examples of virtue"; "She embraced virtue and penance with the same ardor that she had followed her passion."

To recapitulate, writers and their audiences were agreed on the need for *bienséance* and *vraisemblance,* tenets that became increasingly troublesome to reconcile in the eighteenth century.[28] For the time, it was *vraisemblance* that most preoccupied them. One of the principal figures in this reform, as Sorel tells us, was Segrais, Mme de Lafayette's friend and literary adviser. His *Nouvelles Françoises, ou les divertissements de la princesse Aurélie* were published in 1656, a few years before he was drawn into Mme de Lafayette's orbit, but she must have known their principles, if not from having read them, then from having heard them in literary discussions with Segrais. Rich in critical insights (and unfortunately lacking as a realization of those insights), the *Nouvelles Françoises* were no doubt a sourcebook from which Mme de Lafayette drew several of the esthetic values that she incorporated into her works.

The *Nouvelles Françoises* are set in the first year of Louis XIV's majority. The Princesse Aurélie (the Grande Mademoiselle) travels with some companions to her "Château des six tours" (i.e., to her exile at Saint-Fargeau) where the ladies are entertained at balls, promenades, readings, fine conversation, and the like. One of the ladies finds that the countryside puts her in mind of *L'Astrée,* and thereupon the company engages in a discussion of the merits of various novels such as *Polexandre, Le Grand Cyrus, Cléopâtre, Ariane,* and *Cassandre.* "Fine novels," says Aurélie, "are not without instruction, whatever people may say, and especially so since history has been added to them, and when their authors, knowledgeable in the ways of nations, create adventures relating to them and teaching us about them." However, she objects to Frenchified Persians and Greeks, and muses: "The end of this art being to entertain with believable and natural creations, I am astonished that so many persons of wit who have created such respectable Scythians and noble Parthians, have not taken the same pleasure in creating French knights or princes just as accomplished, whose adventures would be no less pleasing." The company then joins in a discussion of Aurélie's reflections.

Frontenie objects that the French would prefer foreign and exotic names like Iphidamante or Orosmane to French ones. Gelonide, however, praises the example of Spanish *novelas,* whose characters have reasonable names like Richard and Lawrence. Uralie thinks such stories would have to be set in the past, it being *invraisemblable* that contemporary heroes and their deeds should have passed unheard of. And, adds Aplanice, why should the heroes always be kings or emperors? Yes, agrees Silerite, look at the stories of Marguerite de Navarre! Here Aurélie intervenes to suggest that each of the six ladies [29] take charge of a day, planning its diversions, and telling a story. Aurélie tells the first story and makes Uralie mistress of the second day. After Boccaccio's *Decameron* and Marguerite de Navarre's *Heptameron,* we have Segrais's *Hexameron.*

At the conclusion of each story, an entertainment follows. There are *questions d'amour,* to wit, "Who is better off, a lover whose mistress is absent but who knows that he is loved, or a lover who does not know whether he is loved?" A pastoral play, *Amarillis,* is performed in a natural stone theater of sylvan setting. There is a debate in which one group defends city life against the other's praise of rustic charm. Gelonide, the city spokesman, bases her arguments chiefly on the advantages of social life, while Silerite vaunts the beauties of nature, the pleasures of simplicity and *repos,* of life *à l'Astrée.* They arrive at no decision, but Segrais, who has a true love of nature in the

Romantic vein, has made Silerite mistress of the sixth and final day, which concludes with a ballet in praise of the *plaisirs de la campagne.*

The stories are set in the Roussillon of the Middle Ages, the England of William the Conqueror, the Burgundy of the Hundred Years' War. The last tale, "Floridon, ou l'amour imprudent," is taken from recent Turkish history, and was told her, Silerite affirms, by the French ambassador to the Ottoman Empire.[30] There are naturally many comments on the art of fiction, and none are more interesting than those of Aurélie herself:

> We have undertaken to tell things such as they are, and not as they ought to be; moreover, it seems to me that the difference between the novel (*roman*) and the *nouvelle* is this: the novel writes these things as propriety (*bienseance*) would have them, and in the manner of the poet, whereas the *nouvelle* must partake more of history, and strive rather to portray things as we ordinarily see them happen, than as our imagination pictures them. (146)

This opinion tallies with the widespread assertion that the poetics of the novel was equivalent to that of the epic and that the novel was merely a prose epic. It also points up the opposition between *nouvelle* and *roman;* length was not the criterium of discrimination, but *vraisemblance.*

Aurélie's story, "Eugénie, ou la force du destin," calls for summary here inasmuch as it presents several traits in common with Mme de Lafayette's novels.

The Comte d'Aremberg arrives in Paris just as his friend the Comte d'Almont is being married. Aremberg immediately falls in love with his friend's bride, sighing: "Alas, what I thought so fantastic is then so true, that man is not free to love or not to love as he wishes. Reason then serves no purpose in regulating our affections when destiny takes a hand. One must become unjust and disregard friendship when a violent passion commands one to." Aremberg enters the Countess' house disguised as "Eugénie," a day-companion (like the Alamir of *Zaïde*) and becomes her confidant. He learns that she really loves Florençal, but has decided to break with him out of respect for her husband: "reason must at last prevail." She arranges a final meeting with Florençal through the jealous "Eugénie," who decides to go to the rendezvous himself. He throws away the Countess' letter to Florençal, which is of course found by Almont, who also decides to attend. Aremberg and Almont, unknown to each other, there engage in play of arms, and Almont is wounded. He dies, Aremberg becomes a monk, and after a suitable period of mourning the Countess marries Florençal: "She took all this time making up her mind, for when she reflected that her friendship for him had been in some way the cause of her first husband's death, she could not think of a second marriage" (134). Her scruples, not very convincingly conveyed, do, with the exception of the marriage, resemble externally those of the Princesse de Clèves.

Although Segrais was not faithful to his particular ideal of portraying things "as we ordinarily see them happen," his emphasis on the *nouvelle* and its *vraisemblance* weighed heavily in the composition of *La Princesse de Montpensier*. From Segrais, Mme de Lafayette evolved a concept of the eternal benefits of restraint that were lacking in the heroic novel. But from the leading exponent of this genre, she took a great deal as well. She adopted the technique of historical setting than which nothing, Mlle de Scudéry believed, better "establishes a well-invented story." She followed Mlle de Scudéry's formula, especially her Anacréon's injunction to choose "a century not so distant that almost nothing in particular is known about it, nor so close that all that has happened is too well-known, yet that is well-known enough to suppose events that an historian could have likely been ignorant of and should not even have told; there is occasion to do much finer things than if one invented everything."[31]

With the single exception of *Zaïde*, which is a special case, Mme de Lafayette remained faithful to this concept. All her novels are set in the reigns of three successive Valois kings, and there is no attempt to foist fiction as fact. The preface of *La Princesse de Montpensier* forthrightly states that the book is fiction and consists of "adventures invented at will." (This was also a prudent means of dissociating her book from a certain defamatory exposé literature, in particular the *Amours du Palais-Royal*, whose "loves" purported to be those of Madame.)

And the preface of *La Princesse de Clèves* (both prefaces are actually called "The Publisher to the Reader"), while eschewing the discredited term *roman* in favor of *livre* or the ambiguous *histoire,* makes no attempt to exploit the new vogue of fictionalized memoirs, largely due to the overwhelming success of the *Lettres Portugaises.* These "letters," anonymously published in 1668, passed for five letters written in passionate accents by a Portuguese nun to her French lover, an officer who had abandoned her. It has lately been demonstrated that they are the work of Guilleragues,[32] but for a long time, and certainly by most seventeenth-century readers, the letters were believed authentic. Readers saw in the heroine's desperate cries of passion "a prodigy of love."[33] What Hermione declaimed in verse, Mariana Alcoforado bared in prose fiction.

Although the vogue for fictionalized memoirs is essentially an eighteenth-century phenomenon, it spread so rapidly that as early as 1709, Steele's *Tatler* carried this warning: "I do hereby give notice to all booksellers and translators whatsoever that the word Memoir is French for a novel."[34] Saint-Réal in particular exploited this vogue, but he was following the example of Mme de Villedieu. In her *Journal Amoureux* (1669), a collection of six *nouvelles historiques,* set under the Valois and drawn from sources like Mézeray, Davila, and Father Anselme (sources that Mme de Lafayette also used), she insisted that her *nouvelles* 'were pure invention. The following year she published the *Annales Galantes,* whose *Avant-propos* enounced principles to which Mme de Lafayette could subscribe:

> I admit that I have added some embellishments to the simplicity of history. . . . When Spanish history tells me that a sovereign Countess of Castille followed a pilgrim of Saint-Jacques [de Compostelle] into France, I presuppose that this great decision was not taken on the spur of the moment; they had to speak and see one another to love that intemperately. Therefore I augment history with some secret meetings and some amorous conversations. If these are not the words they said, they are the ones they should have said . . .[35]

But in addition to, and in spite of these "embellishments," Mme de Villedieu now emphasized the truth and historical accuracy of her collection; they were "historical truths." Mme de Villedieu claimed to be writing a kind of marginal history, "true" or faithful in spirit if not in established fact.

Mme de Lafayette never succumbed to this doubtful temptation. Like her contemporaries, she aspired to *vraisemblance* in fiction, but never in the pretense that she was writing anything but fiction. If she called it *mémoires* or *histoire*, this was to distinguish it from the *roman romanesque*, and because such was the critical terminology of her times. History and fiction were tangential but not interchangeable genres in the mind of Mme de Lafayette, who, after all, wrote real history and memoirs in her *Histoire d'Henriette d'Angleterre* and *Mémoires de la Cour de France pour les années 1688 & 1689*. This is not to say that history is unimportant for Mme de Lafayette, but that the concept of history never coalesces with the concept of fiction. Her simply expressed artistic aim was to create a third fictional mode, neither pure fiction nor embroidered history, but a creation "in which one invents a subject that is not universally known; one embellishes it with several historical traits that support its *vraisemblance* and arouse the reader's curiosity and attention." [36]

La Princesse de Montpensier is the best representative of this nascent genre: from the standpoint of literary history, it is a syncretic work into which Mme de Lafayette incorporated the essence of the reforms under discussion. We have seen that Sorel singled it out for praise, admiring its style in particular, which struck him as being "altogether the tone of fine society." It equally impressed other contemporary readers. Le Sieur Rosteau, in his *Sentimens sur plusieurs auteurs* (under the rubric "Ouvrages d'histoire") also lauded its style: "the surest thing one can say of it is that nothing can be more gallantly written"; he added that Mme de Lafayette was known as "one of the finest wits of our court." Rosteau had heard that the book was a *roman à clef;* the realistic conduct of the characters convinced him that this rumor was true and that the book's preface affirming the contrary should be discounted. [37] The popularity of *La Princesse de Montpensier* is also mentioned in Jean de La Forge's *Le Cercle des Femmes Sçavantes* (1663). In Montfaucon de Villars' *De la délicatesse* (1671; the title means "Concerning Good Taste") there is a subtle analysis of its success. This interesting work consists of five dialogues between two personages, Aliton and Paschase. Noting that novels have gone out of style, Paschase explains that they do not indulge man's penchant for unbridled passion and that they invent amorous fabrications that only imagination authorizes. His interlocutor objects that if this were true, licentious novels should always succeed. Not so, replies the clever Paschase, for

> there is another turn of the heart that only a few people are aware of. Its penchant is to love with abandon *(dérèglement)*, but it does not want this to be believed, nor that it be treated like a libertine. It wants to preserve appearances . . . and it is indignant when it is not treated like a prude. One must know how to flatter its weakness and preserve for it the appearance of strength. . . . Have you read *La Princesse de Montpensier?* It is a little *chef-d'œuvre* that has had an admirable success and will always be read with pleasure, because it excellently flatters so many of the heart's weaknesses. (10–12)

There is no need to prolong this chapter. I might speak of Mme de Lafayette's friend and literary associate, Huet, and his *Traité de l'origine des romans* (1670) with its emphasis on *vraisemblance*, educative value, and historical exactitude in the novel, but Mme de Lafayette possessed all these qualities by 1662. *La Princesse de Montpensier* is not her greatest accomplishment, but it is a work that exemplifies techniques and talents that nurture all her writings: stylistic sobriety and restraint, harsh and tenacious analysis of the heart, and some reverence for morality coupled with (in Stendhal's phrase) the secret "pleasures of pride." [38] The cast is aristocratic, the setting historical, the plot *vraisemblable*. It fits Du Plaisir's nearly Flaubertian dictum: "The slightest action can constitute an admirable action; and all the art of thus imposing a small circumstance is to delineate forcefully, and in a sensitive manner, the characters one speaks of." [39]

CHAPTER 3

La Princesse de Montpensier

I *From Style to Structure*

"While civil war devastated France under the reign of Charles IX, Love did not fail to find its place among so many disorders and to cause many of its own within its Empire." The first sentence of *La Princesse de Montpensier* is perfectly illustrative of the contrapuntal style and structure that inform this short novel more completely and visibly than any other of Mme de Lafayette's fictional endeavors. It presupposes an axiom that may be defined as coercion, under whose aegis love and war are yoked. Love and war are linked in the common wreakage they inflict upon their sufferers, for love troubles a public and private domain in much the same way that war does. Both act within overlapping dominions, the reign of Charles IX and the *empire* of love.

In this sentence (one is tempted to write *sententia*), Mme de Lafayette has consciously played upon the ambiguity of the word *empire*, originally political or course, but recently passed into the *précieux* vocabulary to designate the spell or compulsion under which the lady held her aspiring gallant. The borrowing is an example of metaphoric hyperbole, to be sure, but the compulsive tyranny that characterizes both realms is the organizing principle of this work.

Love's empire extends its rule over all its votaries, and love in turn draws its meaning from the social structure of Mme de Lafayette's novelistic universe. The outward image of an authoritarian society is thus the metaphor of an inward fatalism: both realms are imperious and obscure, and both drive the protagonists toward moral oblivion. This scheme has sociological origins—the intermingling of social and political interests in an aristocratic society—but a sociological approach to the text would be perhaps less fruitful than one might think. For what interests Mme de Lafayette is the psychological repercussions of the scheme, especially when pretense and mask are dropped, in a figurative or in a literal sense. Nevertheless it is true that her novels function in respect to a certain social order, the hierarchies of the *ancien régime*.

The very reciprocity of the twin domains, love and war, explains why *La Princesse de Montpensier*, like all of Mme de Lafayette's works, is not a highly symbolic work, and yet accommodates a symbolism of a special literary variety, that in which the symbol can never be fully separated from what it symbolizes, so interlocking are the two. This "inlaid" symbolism, so to speak, is surely the meaning of Mme de Lafayette's opening sentence. To convey symbolically the interplay of appearance and reality, or duplicity and betrayal, she need have no recourse to contrived imagery, for her images are not artificial constructs of her own devising, but the social realities of an existing society. The intrigues of the court are based on the acceptance of this illusionism, and no character need figuratively mask his game when court games themselves (a ball, for example) permit and even require one to don a real mask. So the interplay between the two dominions, the public and the private, the political and the personal, is presented as a naturally complementary process that operates in a series of counterreverberations.

The story opens quite rapidly with a tableau of the social and political considerations that determine Mlle de Mézières' marriage to the young Prince de Montpensier. With characteristic disdain for physical and even psychological description, Mme de Lafayette marries her heroine in a page and a half to a man for whom she has no affection, and shows her taking an active role in removing the obstacles to her wedding. Mlle de Mézières is at first promised to the Duc du Maine, but she secretly falls in love with his elder brother, the Duc de Guise: "They took great care to hide their love."

As a rich heiress descended from the House of Anjou, Mlle de Mézières is a *parti considérable*, and her impending marriage to a Guise arouses the dynastic cupidity of the Bourbons, who successfully advance their own candidate, the Prince de Montpensier. This reversal fires the indignation of Guise, who now is wounded in his aristocratic pride as well as his love (if indeed the two can be separated). Guise's relatives cannot restrain his anger at this "unbearable affront"; his outbursts are so violent, "even in the presence of the Prince de Montpensier, that a lifelong hatred was born between them." Thus rank, love, and political rivalry become complementary and inseparable considerations that constantly influence one another. It is at this point that Mlle de Mézières exercises her somewhat passive virtue:

> Pressed by her parents to marry this prince, seeing moreover that she could not marry the Duc de Guise, and knowing that it was dangerous to have for a brother-in-law a man she would have wished for a husband, [she] resolved at last to follow the wishes of her people, and entreated M. de Guise no longer to obstruct her marriage. Thus she married the Prince de Montpensier.[1]

Guise's uncles *could not* restrain him; Mlle de Mézières *could not* marry him. The negative modal auxiliaries characterize two tones of the book: a fatalistic mood of acceptance whereby dissimulation drifts into deception and even duplicity, and the impetuous emotional drive that corresponds to it.[2] The end of this expository paragraph is then relinked to the opening motif of war: the Prince de Montpensier takes his new wife to his country estate at Champigny, for Paris is threatened by the Huguenots' resumption of hostilities.

The reader is so rapidly plunged into this schematic and tersely narrated exordium that he hardly recognizes it as such, and yet the principal elements or themes of the novel are clearly recognizable. The style, that of some detached and laconic chronicle, imparts a distinctly historical—and therefore, in the seventeenth-century optic, *vraisemblable*—flavor to the text. This historical tone is achieved in part through an abstract style that renounces imagery, through a brisk succession of imperfects and past definites (the very tenses of historical narration), and a repeated use of demonstrative adjectives ("*this* prince" often in preference to "the Prince de Montpensier" or simply "the prince"; similarly, "*that* beautiful princess" in reference to the heroine) that creates a zone of objectivity between character and reader. We are quite ignorant of the characters' Christian names, and the very formality of the prose rhythms—measured and serene, but never even parenthetically confidential or familiar—sustain the distinct impression of an analytical distance between audience and author.

The intent of this historical objectivity, as I have conjectured, is to vouchsafe the verisimilitude of *La Princesse de Montpensier,* and there results from this imperfectly exploited technique the feeling that we are reading a case history that is sometimes a bit summary where emotionally descriptive abridgments occur. Indeed, *La Princesse de Montpensier* is as much a model or outline of the moral of Mme de Lafayette as it is a fictional work in its own right. To some extent this is true of all her works, for the patterns of *La Princesse de Clèves, La Princesse de Montpensier,* and *La Comtesse de Tende* could all be reduced to a single *question d'amour*: "Married for reasons of convenience, a virtuous young woman falls in love with a man who is not her husband. Will virtue prevail? can it emerge triumphant?" In *La Princesse de Montpensier* we find notations rather than orchestral harmonies; its principal weakness (and I use the word in a relative sense, for inevitably we compare this short work to the work of Mme de Lafayette's maturity, *La Princesse de Clèves*) is perhaps this shorthand compactness that we call "terse" or "dry" according to our reaction to the novel. We read not so much what happens *in* the characters as what happens *to* them, and we can legitimately deplore the sacrifice this entails in psychological acuity.

Despite these strictures, it would be obtuse to categorize *La Princesse de Montpensier* as a minor work to be read only because it contains embryonic negatives of images and themes yet to be developed. Its structure is harmonious to a degree not easily demonstrable in *La Princesse de Clèves,* and its style, whatever our reservations, is already that sublime paradox which constitutes the glory of French Classical prose, an apparently guileless and ordered line that describes nothing but passions and disorders. And in *La Princesse de Montpensier* there is no split between inner and outer reality. Its dual structure, announcing a congruity of form and content, indicates how Classical a work it is.

II *Structure*

The novel is structured entirely upon the interplay of story and history, which is best conveyed, if the reader will bear with me, in a summary of the action. The threatened investment of Paris, we have seen, sends the Princess to Champigny. There ensues an interlude of some two years during which the Prince's intimate and loyal friend, the Comte de Chabanes, devotes himself to cultivating the young girl's nascent perfections: "he made her in a short time into one of the most accomplished persons possible" (7). And Pygmalion-like, he does not fail to fall in love with her.

A truce having been concluded, the Princess' husband returns to Champigny. He is astonished at the transformation of his wife, who has matured into a woman of great beauty, and is somewhat annoyed at the change, for his natural jealousy makes him foresee that "he would not be the only one to find her beautiful." Chabanes, disarming his suspicions, exercising his perfect sincerity (an equivocal virtue, it will be seen), and placing friendship about love, manages to reintroduce the couple to each other, for absence and change have made them virtual strangers.

Once again war intervenes, jolting the tenuous husband-wife relationship in terms whose equal relevance to story and history underscores the coincidence of their pace and progress. For just as Chabanes has effected a reconciliation of sorts, we read the following: "The peace was only apparent. The war recommenced immediately" (9).

The war brings the King's brother, the Duc d'Anjou (the future Henri III) to Loches, the Duc de Guise accompanying him, and yet another fitful truce sends them on an inspection tour of the environs. The princes are young, gallant, and adventurous, and they are roaming one of the loveliest provinces of the realm, the "garden of France," the valleys of the Indre and the Loire. They joyfully lose their way and come to an unknown river.

In a scene that evokes the chivalric mystery of Chrétien's romances and foreshadows the sweetness of Stendhal's *luoghi ameni,* a marvelous encounter takes place. The company perceives several ladies who are watching, from a boat moored in midstream, two nearby salmon fishers. One of the ladies is particularly striking. "This adventure gave renewed joy to these young princes and to everyone of their company. It seemed like an incident from a novel to them" (10). They send horsemen into the shallows within hailing distance to announce M. d'Anjou's sudden desire to cross to the other side. The setting, showing as it does two lovers separated by a physical obstacle they must clear in order to be joined, is typical of Mme de Lafayette's penchant for "natural" imagery. The river is naturally symbolic of a psychological distance or barrier, yet it is not overtly symbolic.[3]

The beautiful lady of the river is of course the Princesse de Montpensier, who blushes to see Guise after three years' time. Her complexion only increases her charms in the eyes of the smitten Duc d'Anjou, who quickly invents a pretext of business on the other bank. The princes linger at Champigny for a stay of several days, much to the surprise, discomfiture, and at last jealous fury of the Prince de Montpensier.

The renewal of hostilities now obliges the Princess to return to Paris and the court, where she again sees Guise. Anjou, taking advantage of an opportune sickness, also returns to Paris, "where the presence of the Princesse de Montpensier was not the least reason that drew him" (14). There is peace once more, and with it, a round of fêtes. This return is necessary for the progress of passion: the court provides opportunity for sentimental intrigue in the form of furtive exchanges and surreptitious meetings. The new lapse of action between the warring factions determines, however, the Princess' banishment to Champigny: no matter how artfully devious she has become (largely thanks to the tutelage of the unhappy Chabanes), her husband does not fail to notice Guise's attentions, and "no longer containing his jealousy, he ordered the Princess his wife to leave for Champigny. This command was a blow to her; nevertheless she had to obey" (23). In this passage we note how the military vocabulary, during interludes of peace, drifts into the sentimental domain.

At this point, better to deceive the Huguenots in preparation for the Saint Bartholomew's Day massacre of 1572, the King disperses Bourbons and Guises to the provinces. Montpensier travels homeward "to finish crushing his wife by his presence," and Guise withdraws to his Cardinal uncle's country residence. Feigning a voyage, he secretly hastens by post to Champigny where he persuades Chabanes to arrange a clandestine meeting with the Princess. Their brief interview ends disastrously when it is surprised by the Prince de Montpensier. This climactic scene is pitched to a fine crescendo that ends in the total emotional rout of the principal characters. The scene is moreover a consummate joining of passion and war, upon which the Saint Bartholomew conspiracy projects what Dina Lanfredini has called a "sinister glare of strife and slaughter."[4]

The naively faithful Chabanes has led Guise through the labyrinth of gallantry. Now, trapped with the Princess, he is unable to extricate himself when the Prince demands entry to his wife's chamber. Chabanes can hastily arrange Guise's escape, but, as the Prince forces the door, he stands like a dead man before the shocked and uncomprehending wrath of his best friend. The characters are emotionally spent, as their poses indicate: the Princess, totally compromised, lies in a half-faint upon some cushions; Chabanes, his honor sullied, slumps despondently against a table; and the Prince, who cannot believe his eyes, throws himself in despair on his wife's bed, crying out the simple and frightening moral of the story, passion's unrelenting descent into chaos and the final disintegration of reality, the erosion of consciousness itself: "What do I see? is it illusion or truth?"

Montfaucon de Villars, Mme de Lafayette's astute contemporary, seized upon this scene to offer a cynical explanation of the book's success:

Montpensier's madness (*démence*) at finding Chabanes with his wife, and the prudence with which he dissimulates his disgrace, suit those husbands who dissimulate the follies of their wives, and find the approval of those whose interests are served by such husbandly conduct. One must not be astonished that this little book, which simultaneously flatters so many weaknesses, has won such a reputation.[5]

The concluding scene of the Saint-Barthélemy massacre may be viewed as the symbolic counterpart of the scene that has just unfolded, inasmuch as it constitutes the assassination of sentiment in *La Princesse de Montpensier*. It is truly a senseless and passionate carnage: the characters' emotions run rife and are transmuted into dark and unspeakable impulses toward death.

The Princess, seized by a fever, remains at Champigny, but the men return once again to Paris, Chabanes to hide there, Montpensier and Guise to take part in the massacre. Chabanes, who is a convert from Protestantism, is brutally murdered, and the Prince de Montpensier, who stumbles by chance upon his friend's body, is secretly jubilant to be avenged by chance. The Duc de Guise, whose family is among the instigators of the massacre, is filled with all the joy of a holocaustal delirium; he abandons all thought of the Princess and finds a new and easier conquest in the person of the shameless Marquise de Noirmoutier.

Both story and history have moved in perfect conjunction toward an ineluctable dénouement of *frenzy* that is emblematic of the anarchic nature of the twin realms of love and war. It is here that the Princess' *mal* reaches its highest degree: "son mal fut venu au dernier point . . ." (32). The term cannot be adequately rendered by a single English word, for in all its apparent banality and literalness, it is really a cluster image that synthesizes a multiplicity of meanings. Its first meaning in this context refers to the heroine's illness, but beyond this it alludes to the *evil* nature of passion, to the *harm* done the characters, the sense of *rue* the Princess feels, and the *wrongdoing* of her actions. It already has the terrible richness that we associate with Racinian usage.[6]

The Princess' fever breaks, and reason returns ("La raison lui revint") as if to allow a brief respite in which to survey the destruction about her. There are faintly elegiac notes in the final passages, and novel closes on the tone of a moral exemplum, with characteristically negative phrasing:

> She could not withstand the grief of having lost her husband's regard, her lover's heart, and the most perfect friend that ever was. She died within a few days, in the flower of her youth, one of the most beautiful princesses in the world, who no doubt would have been the happiest, if virtue and prudence had guided all her actions. (33)

III. *The Characters*

i. The Princess and Chabanes

In using the term exemplum to describe the tone of the closing pages of *La Princesse de Montpensier,* I did not mean thereby to imply the presence of any moralistic overtones in Mme de Lafayette's novel. Moral strictures there may be, but these remain implicit, and, save the final sentence, which is cast in the form of a supposition, there is no moral judgment of the title character. Nowhere in the text do authorial interventions occur, and its fundamental objectivity is consistently respected. Nevertheless, we may wonder at one unstated change that Mme de Lafayette has made in the historical record. The Princesse de Montpensier, unlike the Princesse de Clèves, is not an invented character: Mme de Lafayette probably found her in Davila's *Histoire des guerres civiles de France.*[7] Historically, Mlle de Mézières was sixteen at the time of her marriage, but Mme de Lafayette has significantly made her thirteen,[8] thus suggesting her adeptness, even at this age, at the dissimulation necessary to emotional survival in her social world. This discreet change has its implications, although it is never implied that Mlle de Mézières is naturally vicious or that her conduct flows from her nature. Mme de Lafayette never entertained any such simplistic or causal views of passion, whose most characteristic and terrifying features are that it has no past and suffers no defense. Thus the question of virtue becomes problematical, as *La Princesse de Clèves* amply demonstrates. Mme de Lafayette is less interested in exploring moral flaws than in observing the patterns of discontinuity that passion engenders.

The Princess' initial success at dupery, when she and Guise hide their love, is rather innocent, and may be credited to a commensensical grasp of what is socially acceptable. Her later acceptance of Montpensier and her plea to Guise to set no obstacle in the way of her marriage is a bit more political, inasmuch as it involves an appraisal of what is socially feasible. Morally, it remains an act of passive virtue, and this passivity is the key to her character. Given her age, it is hard to see how it might be otherwise. This very docility in the hands of her self-appointed tutor, Chabanes, is what permits him to make of her a polished young woman in such a short time, although a precocious social agility is also at work. It is at the same time a quality that is manifested through *confiance*, or trust, in her relationship with Chabanes. The word reoccurs with a notable frequency, and the reader of *La Princesse de Clèves* cannot help recalling that Mme de Clèves was taught by her mother always to cultivate an *extrême défiance de soi-même*—an extreme mistrust of oneself (248). Her distrust is self-vigilance and contrasts with the Princesse de Montpensier's *confiance*, which is submissive and somewhat flaccid.

The Princess' trust in Chabanes is so complete that she tells him of her former love for Guise. There remains, she confides, only enough of her inclination to make her scorn any other suitor. Chabanes, who has fallen passionately in love with her, interprèts this avowal as an example of her virtue, of "dispositions so opposed to the weakness of gallantry" (7) that he does not reflect upon the nature of that remaining "inclination." What she has told him, in effect, is that she can love no other man than Guise. This is the true extent of her virtue, whose sole guarantor is lack of opportunity.

Chabanes never fully grasps the import of her confession and is powerless to shield himself from her scorn, to which he knowingly exposes himself. At first his reaction—he is "much older" than she—is naturally to conceal his love from the young Princess: "If he was not the master of his heart, he was of his actions" (7). But the passage of time, as so often is the case in Mme de Lafayette, is corrosive of resolve and purpose: "Love did to him what it does to everyone: it gave him the desire to speak out, and after all the struggles that one suffers on such occasions, he dared to tell her that he was in love, having braced himself to bear the rage with which that Princess' pride menaced him" (7).

Instead of the rigors of her virtue, Chabanes finds that he must suffer something far worse, for the Princess receives his profession of love with indifference and unresponsiveness:

> She did not take the trouble to be angry with him. In a few words she pointed out to him the differences in their social condition and age, his particular knowledge of the inclination she had had for the Duc de Guise, and above all what he owed to the friendship and trust of her husband the Prince. The Count thought he would die at her feet of shame and sorrow. (7–8)

The Princess promises to forget his avowal and to continue to regard him as a friend. Chabanes will not even be accorded a measure of scorn, and the Princess, faithful to her word, treats him with a familiar contempt that transforms him into a sentimental lackey. He has become a kind of animated object in her eyes, and she does not scruple to speak again to him of the Duc de Guise, whose exploits in the wars make her happy that he is "worthy of the feelings that she had had for him. All these marks of trust, which had been so dear to the Count became unbearable to him" (8). Chabanes' rebuff demonstrates for us one of the verities of love according to Mme de Lafayette, its single-minded egotism, before which the generosity and trust of a Chabanes are trifling considerations. To the selfishness of love, only self-interest is sincere, and Chabanes' inborn nobleness of soul, his *générosité*, is mere ingenuousness. Similarly, Chabanes' conversion to the Catholic party out of friendship for the Prince de Montpensier is so conspicuously lacking in political motivation that its sincerity is doubted by Catherine de Médicis (6). Love and politics are linked in self-interest, and during the Saint-Barthélemy massacre Chabanes pays with his life for his artlessness. Set apart as foils of disguise and undisguise, the Princess and Chabanes are nevertheless paired by passion in one supremely important respect: they are both destined to derogation in the eyes of themselves and others.

Chabanes' sense of self-respect has soon dwindled to a grateful servitude, and commensurately, the Princess' treatment of her faithful companion becomes increasingly cavalier. The pathos of his love is heightened when we consider that he is much older than his blithe young Princess, who sees perhaps only the ludicrousness of his state. When Anjou and Guise leave the Prince de Montpensier at Champigny in a rage of jealousy and hatred, Chabanes is reduced to allaying the latter's suspicions on behalf of the Princess, a pathetic effort to demonstrate the sincerity and disinterestedness of his love. He ventures to ask her about her emotions upon seeing Guise: "She informed him that she had been disturbed by the shame of the memory of the inclination she had formerly shown him; that she had found him much handsomer than he was in those days . . ." (13–14). "Shame" is to be understood here as expressing no penitent regret; her blush upon seeing him again is much more revealing of that *honte*. Chabanes worriedly promotes her intention never to embark upon an adventure, but the Princess has little thought for him. In the following passage, we can imagine an anxious Chabanes at the side of a musing Princesse de Montpensier, abstractedly gazing into the distance and taking little note of her companion: "The Princesse de Montpensier, still continuing her way with him, barely replied to what he told her of his love, and only considered in him the quality of best possible friend, without deigning to do him the honor of noticing that of lover" (10).

In Paris, Guise boldly declares his love for the Princess at the very moment when her husband enters the room; she is so surprised and confused that her expression again betrays her emotions, and the Prince's jealousy redoubles. Guise and the Princess must now hide their feelings even more carefully, but it is not long before "their hearts effortlessly resumed a road that was not unknown to them" (17). The Princess is not without remorse at her illicit "commerce" with Guise, but like all the characters of *La Princesse de Montpensier,* she is weak. The self-will of the Princess is a fragile thing: "These thoughts made her take new resolutions, but they were dissipated the next day at the sight of the Duc de Guise" (18). This novel remains constantly chaste, and it is precisely because of that chasteness that the sense and importance of physical presence are overwhelming.

Despite his reassurances, Guise's favor with Madame (the Duc d'Anjou's sister) makes the Princess jealous. Jealousy has many uses in Mme de Lafayette, not the least of which is to make passion burn more openly. The Princess' true feelings, which she has refused to recognize by taking refuge in the subterfuge of her virtue, are now laid bare by jealousy. The news of Madame's affection for Guise "was not indifferent to her and made her feel that she took more interest in the Duc de Guise than she thought" (16). Jealously invariably accompanies love and stirs the turmoil of desire. Seeking out passion behind its mask of virtuous reticence and aristocratic mien, jealousy cajoles it to exposure and ruin.

This is the meaning of the ballet that the King has organized in honor of his marriage to the daughter of Emperor Maximilian. The characters are literally forced into a performance that dramatizes their situation as it strips them of their masks. Costumed as Moors, Guise and four other gentlemen dance an *entrée* with the Duc d'Anjou.[9] Shortly before the ballet begins, Guise exchanges a few words with the Princess, and is noticed by the Prince de Montpensier. After the dance, the Princess sees a mask in Moorish costume approaching, and assuming it is Guise, she blurts out in confusion: "This evening, have eyes only for Madame, I will not be jealous, I order you to do so, I am being watched, don't come near me" (18). She hurriedly withdraws, leaving a "thunderstruck" Duc d'Anjou behind her.

Now Guise has carefully hidden his love from Anjou, knowing how disastrous it might be to have for a rival the first prince of the realm. Deceived by the complexity of her own pretense, symbolized by the Duke's mask, the Princess has unwittingly exposed her lover to the royal wrath. But this is more than an involuntary revelation, for it signifies all the confusion and breakdown of forms and appearances that passion causes in a moral and social order. The terms involuntary and voluntary moreover become meaningless when chaos reigns; and chaos reigns precisely when appearance and reality merge, when masks are penetrated. Thus passion is self-betrayal and humiliation.

Anjou, who has no difficulty in understanding the Princess' words, seeks out Guise with murder in his heart:

"It is too much," he told him, "to dare lift your eyes to my sister and to take my mistress from me. Respect for the King prevents me from an outburst; but remember that the loss of your life may be the least thing with which I shall one day punish your temerity." (19)[10]

Anjou fans the King's ire and ruins Guise's chances for Madame's hand. The King openly insults Guise the next day. Anjou continues in his rage to speak the unspeakable truths that convention and seemliness forbid and veil. He tells the Princess that he knows all and warns her that Guise "is deceiving you, Madame, and is sacrificing you to my sister, as he sacrificed her to you. He is a man capable only of ambition . . ." (20).

The Princess learns too late how true his words are. Her immediate preoccupation is to know her secret in the hands of a powerful man whom she has mistreated and to learn that Guise has deceived her. To reassure her and to make the best of an impossible situation, Guise abruptly announces his engagement to the Princesse de Portien (and thereby renounces any hope for Madame). Thus he restores appearances, and now the Princess is deceived by deception; the lovers are briefly reconciled, but the Prince de Montpensier forces his wife's return to

Champigny. There she summons Chabanes to inform him (not request him) that he is to bear letters between herself and Guise: "It was the last blow for the Comte de Chabanes, to see that his mistress wanted him to serve his rival and that she made this proposal as if it were a pleasant task for him. He was so absolutely master of himself that he concealed all his feelings from her" (23–24). The reader can savor the full irony of "master of himself"; Chabanes no longer has any will of his own and meekly agrees to carry the letters. The Princess is so totally absorbed in her love, and so totally oblivious and insensitive to the wretched Chabanes that she reads the Duke's letters to him, as well as her own "tender and gallant" replies. When he ventures to remind the Princess of his own love, she is piqued and testily reduces him to silence. He leaves Champigny in a huff.

The Princess began to repent having so little spared a man over whom she had so much power; and, as she could not accept losing him, not only because of her friendship for him, but also in the interests of her love, to which he was quite necessary, she sent word that she absolutely wished to speak to him one more time, and that afterwards, she left him free to do as he pleased. One is very weak when one is in love. The Count returned and in less than an hour, the beauty of the Princesse de Montpensier, her vivacity [*esprit*], and a few obliging words made him more submissive than he had ever been, and he even gave her some letters that he had just received from the Duc de Guise. (25)

Mme de Lafayette's little aphorism about love and weakness is wonderfully understated. Chabanes is so subjugated to the Princess' bidding that he can no longer think or act for himself. His only impulse is to remain in her presence and suffer any humility; his love has turned him from preceptor into puppet. As for the Princess, her "friendship" for Chabanes exchanged for exploitation, the satisfaction of desire occupies her entirely. When Chabanes brings news of Guise's wish to see her, her reaction is characteristically double. As in the passage just quoted, her first thought is for morality (in other words, a rapidly vanishing seemliness, an appearance); this soon gives way to practical considerations more intimately connected with her passion (*her* reality):

At first her love pictured the joy she would have in seeing a man she loved so tenderly. But, when she thought how much this act was contrary to her virtue, and that she could only see her lover by letting him in at night without her husband's knowledge, she found herself in a terrible state. (26)

The abject Chabanes, divining the Princess' uncertainty, tells her of the perils she is courting, and then, still nourishing the illusion that his impartiality may gain him some favor, offers to bring Guise to her apartments. The Princess' reaction is swift and visceral: "But what way and how?"

When Chabanes sets off to fetch Guise, the Princess suffers an emotional blackout:

The Princesse de Montpensier was left so perturbed that it was some time before she came to. Her first impulse was to have the Comte de Chabanes called back and to forbid him to bring the Duc de Guise; but she had not the strength to do so. She thought that without recalling him, she had only not to let the bridge down. She believed that she would maintain this resolution. When the hour of the assignation approached, she could no longer resist the desire to see a lover she thought so worthy of her. . . . (27)

This passage is one of a type in which Mme de Lafayette excels in conveying, through syntactical rhythms that are nearly irrespirable, the welter of confusion that grips and transfixes her heroines: "She thought"—"She believed"—"Her first impulse was to resist"—are so many unavailing lunges against the snares of passion triumphant. Finally, "She could no longer resist." The virtue of virtue is to resist, and in the harsh perspective of Mme de Lafayette, it is meaningless unless achieved in refusal and denial.

ii.   Guise

Love does not ennoble any of the characters of *La Princesse de Montpensier,* and this is especially true of the Duc de Guise, whose personality is the least appealing of any in the novel (with the possible exception of the Prince de Montpensier, who is really a one-dimensional character). Born into a great family, destined to become chief of the dreaded *Ligue* and to be surnamed *le balafré* ("scarface"), Guise is acutely conscious of the panoply of power and privilege attached to his birth. All of his actions must be interpreted in light of this status, so that ultimately none of them is disinterested. Mme de Lafayette has, in addition, chosen to emphasize his rather frequent disgraces in matters where aristocratic pride is at stake. He receives demeaning insults from the Duc d'Anjou, and from the King himself. At the very outset of the novel he must bear the indignity of seeing the Bourbons snatch away the wealthy Mlle de Mézières.

In this it is clear that considerations of rank are never separable from his initially spontaneous love of Mlle de Mézières. Moreover, the first mention of the Duke's character, before the real love intrigue begins, concerns his ambitiousness: "he did not yet have so much ambition as he since had . . ." (5). If we assume that this ambitiousness will be joined to his enduring hatred for Montpensier, it follows that winning the Prince's wife is as much an act of vengeance (stemming from humiliation) as it is an act of passion. The Princess too seems to love on somewhat analogous grounds, for Mme de Lafayette stresses how "worthy" of herself the heroine finds Guise. Love is never *only* itself, or pure; it is always *intéressé*.

Within the perspective of *La Princesse de Montpensier's* structure, it would not be exaggerated to argue that Guise's military vigor (whose deeds keep him in the reader's eye while the narrative fastens on the Princess' adolescence) and his amatory prowess are of the same cloth. Certainly the word "exploit" would apply equally, and we know that Don Juan is as skillful at swordplay as he is at seduction. Mme de Lafayette's inquiry is more concerned with the effects of passion than its inscrutable origins, but her text's sober allusiveness does not conceal its affinity with Molière's play.[11] *Dom Juan* comes only three years after *La Princesse de Montpensier,* and while Guise does not possess the conscious effrontery of Molière's character, who has in sexual matters "the ambition of conquerors, who perpetually fly from victory to victory, and cannot resolve to curb their desires" (Act I, sc. ii), he is fickle, and like Don Juan, exerts a powerful fascination over women of the highest station, notably the King's sister.

The river meeting with the Princess is framed as an adventure and comes during a lull in the fighting. As love and war overlap throughout the novel, we are tempted to interpret the chance encounter as yet another obstacle or conquest in the path of the glorious Duke. Guise *probes* almost at once, telling the Princess, with the certainty that his words will not be understood by the others, that "his heart had not changed at all" (12). Upon leaving Champigny, Anjou abruptly asks his opinion of the Princess, and Guise is obliged to dissimulate, knowing how dangerous it would prove to figure as the rival of the King's brother. Now given the temperament of Guise, his love, weaned on humiliation and high aspiration, can only batten on the rivalry of such an illustrious personage who is so affected at the sight of the Princess, and who "tried to make the Duc de Guise agree that he felt the same thing; but this Duke, who was beginning to make a serious matter of his love, refused to admit anything" (13).

This impression is confirmed by Guise's forthright "attack" in Paris; his declaration is precipitated by a passion so strong that "neither your *severity*, nor the *hatred* of M. le Prince de Montpensier, nor the *rivalry* of the first prince of the realm can take from it an instant of its force" (15, my italics). His passion, he asserts, exists independently and in spite of these considerations, but who can believe that it is not the other way round? His triple motivation—an obstacle, revenge, ambition—holds in this one sentence.

In defense of Guise, we may say that he is a man of action and not a person who questions the nature of his love (nor does the Princess until it is so late that she can barely do so); it is this lack of consciousness regarding his purposes that prevents us from calling him a Don Juan, even in moments when he appears most hypocritical. When he sacrifices all hope for a dazzling match on the altar of his love for the Princess, is this not the sort of sacrifice we should skeptically enclose in quotation marks? For sacrifice can scarcely be legitimized by force of circumstance. The Princess exults in this proof of her lover's sincerity and devotion, but the Duke's response is less conclusive; in fact, it is ambiguous: "The Duc de Guise, who wished that love should at least reward him for what he was losing in the matter of fortune, pressed the Princess to grant him a private hearing . . ." (21).

Several furtive meetings ensue in the course of which Guise convinces the Princess of the integrity of his love. Then she is sent to Champigny and the lovers arrange to correspond, using Chabanes as intermediary. There is a brief lull in the action until Guise experiences a "violent desire" to see the Princess; this desire, we read, is provoked by *"love and idleness"* (25), an association with inescapable implications. Stripped of favor at court, his hopes for a brilliant marriage dashed, Guise turns toward the apparently accessible Princess almost like a *divertissement* to his disoccupation. Stepping through breaches in the walls of the castle and crossing its drawbridge, the image of Guise the lover is in slow transition to that of Guise the warrior. Once his abortive attempt at seduction is frustrated, he returns to Paris in search of easier and more violent conquests: the bloody massacre of unsuspecting Huguenots and the favors of a profligate marquise whom he loves with "unbridled passion" (32).

As in *La Princesse de Clèves,* the already objective tone of *La Princesse de Montpensier* becomes still more removed and distant in the closing pages. The characters, blurred by the distortions of passion, are engulfed in the chaos of history. The final paragraphs stand apart like some epilogue in which time and action have been telescoped for the reader's benefit and instruction.

The outlines of *La Princesse de Montpensier* foreshadow the greater substance and achievement of Mme de Lafayette's masterpiece. Chabanes' double role as mentor and confessor will be shared by Mme de Chartres and M. de Clèves. The ambitious Guise will become the disquieting Nemours of past triumph and inconstancy. The Princesse de Clèves will have a conscience and consciousness denied her predecessor; and her virtue will stand at the very center of passionate disorder. Jealousy, the inconstancy of love, the depredations of time, and above all, the illogic of reason, will mediate the characters' fate. But like *La Princesse de Clèves,* like *La Comtesse de Tende,* Mme de Lafayette's first novel ends in death and disenthrallment.

CHAPTER 4

Zaïde

I Background

The reader whose first acquaintance with Mme de Lafayette was *La Princesse de Clèves* will be surprised and disappointed upon opening *Zaïde*. His reaction will be perfectly understandable, for this book is both the longest of Mme de Lafayette's fictional endeavors and the least characteristic of her art, and it is really no novel at all, but a romance. There is psychological analysis to be found in it, and it is thematically related to Mme de Lafayette's other works, but it does not follow the vein that she had first exploited in *La Princesse de Montpensier* and continued in *La Princesse de Clèves* and *La Comtesse de Tende*, that of somber linear development, the reader's attention fixed upon a narrative "thread" never lost even in the famous digressions of her masterpiece.

Annoyingly, *Zaïde* is the only work of Mme de Lafayette's that her contemporaries unequivocally attributed to her. Segrais, under whose name *Zaïde* was published, wrote that his sole contribution concerned its structure, in which "the rules of Art are observed with great accuracy." [1] Huet wrote that he had "first hand knowledge" of Mme de Lafayette's authorship and had "often seen Mme de Lafayette busy with this work." [2]

If read in the order of publication of her novels, *Zaïde* appears to mark a step backwards. Structurally, it is full of awkward and tiresome flashbacks, making for disjointed development; and thematically, there are innumerable concessions to a fashion that Mme de Lafayette seemed to have gone beyond, that of the *roman romanesque* with its shipwrecks, mistaken identities, and Frenchmen in exotic masquerade. All these

Scuderian trappings, and more, are present in *Zaïde*. These shortcomings are attributable to a literary tradition that went back nearly a century before *Zaïde*'s publication to the *nouvelle mauresque*. This was not a period genre like the pastoral, but a type of novel—the Hispano-Moorish tale—that has always occupied a minor niche in French literature, from *Zaïde* to Chateaubriand's *Aventures du dernier Abencérage* and Barrès' *Du sang, de la volupté et de la mort*.[3]

Spain was much in vogue in seventeenth-century France, especially in the early decades, which saw French translations of Cervantes and Montemayor, and, in 1608, of Ginés Perez de Hita's *Historia de los Vandos de los Zegries y Abencerrages* as *Les Guerres Civiles de Grenade*. Perez de Hita's work, drawn in part from Spanish *romances*, was a vast "historical" panorama of the last days of the Moorish empire in Granada. It met with considerable success in the Hôtel de Rambouillet and provided the historical, if not the novelistic framework for *Zaïde*.[4] The popularity of these adventures was not exhausted even in Mme de Lafayette's time, for Madeleine de Scudéry's *Almahide* of 1660 was inspired by Perez de Hita, as were several other books.[5] And Louis XIV himself had contributed to interest in Spain by wedding the Infanta in 1660.

Zaïde, as we have seen, was a collective enterprise. Its success, to judge from its printings, was not as striking as that of *La Princesse de Montpensier*, and several readers, Bussy-Rabutin, for example, criticized its *invraisemblances*.[6] Its greatest success seems to have come in the eighteenth century when it was re-published nine times and acclaimed by La Harpe as marking the beginning of the French novel. The first of its two volumes was prefaced by Huet's *Treatise on the Origin of Novels*, a ponderous affair wherein Huet asserts that "Novels are fictitious stories of love adventures, written in prose for the pleasure and instruction of readers." The value of the novel is seen as consisting in its ethical worth (by which Huet means its moral didacticism). Underscoring the novel's parentage with the epic, he says that whereas the poem stresses the *merveilleux*, the novel stresses the *vraisemblable* and has more "episodes." The subject of the novel is love. As dull and vapid as many of these premises may be, they are incorporated to a large degree in *Zaïde*.[7]

II Questions d'amour

A modern subtitle of *Zaïde* might be "Pathologies of Love," for the novel is nothing more than a series of loosely connected adventures that, in spite of a happy ending, demonstrate these propositions: love is constancy, love is jealousy, love is betrayal. Theses might be a better word, for *Zaïde,* following a brief sketch of the political situation in ninth-century Spain (and preparing the intertwining of political and love intrigue), immediately plunges the reader into an abstract discussion of unhappiness in love. In a page that noticeably bears the mark of *littérature de salon,* Mme de Lafayette and her collaborators produce a conversation between Consalve, a wandering nobleman, and Alphonse, a recluse whom he has chanced to meet near the latter's *désert* by Tarragon:

"The crowning misfortune," exclaimed [Alphonse], "is to have to find fault with oneself, to have dug the abyss into which one has fallen, to have been unfair and unreasonable; finally, it is to have been the cause of the calamities that overwhelm one!"
"I can see," said Consalve, "that you suffer from the ills that you mention; but how different they are from those one suffers when, without deserving it, one is deceived, betrayed and abandoned by all one cherished most!" (40)

Behind the abstract and indirect phrasing of each character, there lies of course a story; sensing that Consalve too has been unhappy in love, and shares his distaste for society, Alphonse invites him to share his solitary existence. Consalve accepts.

One morning while strolling on the beach, Consalve and Alphonse find a beautiful woman—Zaïde—unconscious, having been washed ashore by a storm at sea. Consalve, who is obviously seeking solace from an unhappy love affair, is distressed, gazing at Zaïde's lovely countenance, to feel himself "surprised" by the graceful proportions of her features, "astonished by the beauty of her lips and the whiteness of her bosom," and so totally "charmed" that he exclaims: "How fortunate am I in my distress, that the cruel experience I have of women's unfaithfulness protects me from ever loving another one!" (44). Yet as Zaïde is nursed back to health and reunited with her lady companion Félime, Consalve finds himself irresistibly drawn to her presence. "What interest," he demands, "can I possibly take in the misfortunes of a person that I do not know at all?" He insists to Alphonse that it is only compassion that he feels for Zaïde. Moreover, the fact that Consalve and Zaïde do not speak the same language does not help him decipher his sentiments. Consalve's language of course is Spanish and Zaïde's, we eventually learn, is Greek.

This language barrier is first of all one of those insipid inventions in which *romanesque* novelists delighted, and functionally it serves as a device for suspending the resolution of the main plot's love interest. But its immediate function, as concerns part I of *Zaïde*, is to demonstrate the irrational and even supralinguistic nature of love: not knowing Zaïde, and indeed lacking the very means (language) of knowing her, Consalve is convinced that his feelings can have nothing to do with love. For Consalve, spiritual inhabitant of *Tendre-sur-Reconnoissance*, has always believed that love is something that *comes to be*; he cannot therefore believe or recognize his true feelings for Zaïde, a person he does not know. But Mme de Lafayette will demonstrate that love has no language, or rather, that it is its own language.

When Consalve comes to believe from Zaïde's incessant tears that she is mourning a lost lover, or at least lamenting his absence, he experiences jealousy, that agonizing emotion that grips his heart in which "love had not yet declared itself" (48). Moreover, when Consalve is also convinced from Zaïde's gestures that he resembles this absent lover, he is consumed by the green-eyed monster; then he cries out that "jealousy alone has made me feel that I was in love" (50). Having admitted the undeniable evidence of his love for Zaïde, Consalve can now confide to Alphonse his true identity and the reasons that led him to abandon society.

Literally, Mme de Lafayette has shown us two persons, unknown to each another, not speaking the same tongue, and each ignorant of the other's social rank. Yet none of this has prevented them from falling in love, for love is inexplicable in its immediacy: it knows no barriers. The long flashback that now intervenes is intended further to discredit the a priori concept of love as knowledge. (This concept, incidentally, was one expressed in the first volume of *Clélie*, which we know Mme de

Lafayette read.) This section is really the moral of *Zaïde's* first sixteen pages.

The "Story of Consalve" briefly sketches Consalve's eminent position in the court of Leon, his friendship with a gentleman of his suite, Don Ramire, and the special favor bestowed upon him by the King's son, Prince Don Garcie. These friends often twit Consalve for his supposed insensitivity in matters of the heart, and he in turn blames them for their fickleness: "You will never convince me that you can be in love with a person whose face you barely know. . . ." To which the Prince replies: "we know their beauty, and in love, that is most impotrant."

Consalve insists that for him knowledge and esteem must invariably precede love, that these ingredients constitute its foundation. He is astonished by Don Ramire's contention that for him there would be even greater pleasure in becoming "master of a heart" that was already in love: his *gloire* and love would be doubly satisfied at winning a mistress from a rival. (Don Ramire, along with Alamir, provides the link between the psychology of Guise in *La Princesse de Montpensier* and Nemours in *La Princesse de Clèves*.) Don Garcie interrupts once more as Mme de Lafayette's spokesman:

I would be incapable of falling in love with a person I had known for a long time, and if I am not surprised at first, I cannot be touched. I believe that natural inclinations are felt in the first moments, and that passions that come only with time cannot be called true passions. (54)

Consalve jokingly retorts that he must then take care that the Prince see his young sister Hermenesilde before her beauty is fully formed, for should the Prince fall in love with her, the disparity in their rank would prevent their marriage, and Consalve would thus have the displeasure of seeing his sister become the Prince's mistress.

The name of Nugna Bella, one of the court's great beauties, is then mentioned. The Prince is not affected by her charms, having grown up with her. Don Ramire is not tempted either, for he "would have no one to expell from her heart"; as for Consalve, he blushingly admits that he could love her if he "knew her better." The Prince is delighted and procures him the opportunity of seeing Nugna Bella.

From here the plot unfolds quite mechanically in terms of the rather summary psychology of the characters: the Prince does not fail to fall in love with Hermenesilde and out of embarrassment, conceals his love from Consalve, making Don Ramire his confidant; Nugna Bella, observing the decline of Consalve's favor with the Prince, responds to the advances of Don Ramire, who has the triple pleasure of loving Nugna Bella, displacing his friend in her heart, and acquiring the Prince's favor. Consalve is doomed to betrayal by the political ambitions of Nugna Bella and Don Ramire on the one hand, by the passion of the Prince and Hermenesilde on the other. The Prince has little difficulty in consenting to his friend's exile: "he was so ashamed of everything that he was doing to me that my presence constituted a continual reproach to his weakness" (77). The intertwined egotisms of love and ambition brook no disinterested considerations. Moreover, every character in Consalve's story, save Consalve himself, is touched by ambition to some degree, and their sentiments can never be evaluated in themselves. Thus they are productive of betrayal and duplicity, for they are never fully separable from intrigue.

So it is that Consalve, betrayed and abandoned by all that he most cherished, decides to "renounce forever wordly commerce and end my life in some forsaken place" (82). Now Consalve's betrayal by Nugna Bella engenders indignation at first and finally melancholy, but significantly, not jealousy. And therefore, implies Mme de Lafayette, he did not really know love. Consalve's bitter experience leads him to an attitude of complete mistrust of love and women. Yet love is unreason, and following its unseizable "logic," misogyny's neophyte falls jealously in love with an *unknown* woman, Zaïde. Jealousy and affection are so intimately linked in Mme de Lafayette that one almost expects to find in the text the expression *tomber jaloux de quelqu'un.*

Ah, Alphonse, what a terrible thing jealousy is! Ah, Don Garcie, you were right: the only passions are those that strike us straight off and take us by surprise; the others are only liaisons to which we voluntarily bear our hearts. True inclinations tear our hearts from us in spite of ourselves. . . . (88)

The first part of Mme de Lafayette's demonstration has been

accomplished. The theory of love based on knowledge has been destroyed and a capital element in the evolution of every true passion, jealousy, has been introduced. It is now developed in the "Story of Alphonse and Bélasire," which teaches us that while jealousy is the sign of love, it is not its guarantor. The story will hold great interest for Consalve, whose unfounded jealousy continues unabated and is indeed exacerbated by Zaïde's precipitate and mysterious departure.

III *More Lessons in Love*

The "Story of Alphonse and Bélasire" constitutes the second long flashback of part I of *Zaïde*. It is largely episodic— Alphonse is less a true character than a metaphor of the dangers attending Consalve's love for Zaïde, and after his tale is concluded he is not heard from again—and in particular it is admonitory, for Consalve has now reached an emotional stage that Alphonse has gone beyond, and can view with objective maturity. He too, at the point where his story commences, had suffered

only through the fault of others and not my own . . . I had experienced everything grievous that the infidelity and inconstancy of women can make one suffer. Thus I was very far from desiring to love any woman. . . . I had no repugnance for marriage, but the experience I had of women made me resolve never to marry a beautiful one; and after having suffered so much from jealousy, I had no wish to expose myself [like M. de Clèves] to the jealousy of both lover and husband. (106)

But Alphonse is not immune from love, and like Don Ramire, he responds to obstacles, not the challenge of evincing another lover, but of conquering an insensitive heart. Thus he is almost fated to love Bélasire, in spite of his fear of her beauty, for he has a sure way of ascertaining that she has never loved: " 'No,' she told me, 'I know none of the feelings of love. 'What! not even jealousy?' said I. 'No, not even jealousy,' she replied. 'Ah, madame, if that is so then I am convinced that you have never had an inclination for anyone' " (108).
Stimulated by the desire to conquer Bélasire's insensitivity,

Alphonse has at least the equivocal pleasure of seeing her experience "feelings over which she had no control." Moreover, Alphonse has the misfortune to be an absolutist in love, and the projections of his imagination, tending toward the future, represent the horrors of being jealous in marriage. More important, his will to mastery also extends to the past: to taste the full measure of his triumph, he entreats Bélasire to tell him all that her past suitors had done for her:

> She told me that the most perservering were those toward whom she had been the most distant, and that she had never liked the Comte de Lare, who had loved her until his death. I don't know why, after what she told me, I was more curious about what concerned the Comte de Lare than the others . . . I was touched by a sort of jealousy. (111)

Alphonse is instantly seized by a morbid and imperious desire to know *all,* and nothing Bélasire can say will appease his jealousy. Thus an intellectual malady is born that will destroy his love and more. Alphonse has now found an obstacle that he cannot overcome; it is unsurmountable because it is in the past and dead, therefore impervious to time, change, or knowledge. In the beginning, what was inaccessible elicited and sustained his love; now another inaccessibility plunges it into despair. Alphonse can never attain certainty, and the very thought that the Count might have believed himself, however mistakenly, loved by Bélasire gives him no rest.

Alphonse forces Bélasire to tell and retell every incident of the Count's attentions to her, but the "places where she went into detail were unbearable to me; I thought that she certainly had a great recollection of the actions of a man who had been indifferent to her" (115). Alphonse's jealousy becomes self-hatred and distrust of Bélasire. It relentlessly evolves into a monstrous frenzy that drives his mistress to the convent, convinced that "one cannot be happy in loving someone" (123), and leads Alphonse to kill his best friend. Its ravages clearly prefigure the Proustian treatment of love and jealousy in *Un Amour de Swann,* the torments that Proust describes as "reciprocal torture." Alphonse, like Swann after him, will be forever ignorant of the past of his Odette, and will suffer from the passion that extends a promise of knowledge while constantly denying it. Alphonse is torn between passion and logic and cries out "I could see that I was wrong; but it was beyond my power to be sensible" (115). This is the lesson of every love in Mme de Lafayette's sharp optic.

At the conclusion of the "Story of Alphonse and Bélasire," Consalve has presumably learned the perils of jealousy. He sets out to join the wars against the Saracens, and with the secret hope of finding Zaïde. He does indeed see her again, but before the lovers can communicate (Zaïde has learned Spanish during her absence), Consalve is forced to return to court by Don Garcie's men. So ends part I of Zaïde.

The two stories just examined form the bulk of the narrative in part I and are designed as a commentary on the principal action, the love of Consalve and Zaïde. Because of their length they stand as stories complete in themselves, and there is a temptation to view them as constituting in themselves the substance of part I, and as reflecting (as disconnected tales) the rather disjointed structure of the novel as a whole. But in reality they function—in an ungainly way—much as the digressions of La Princesse de Clèves, as admonitory gestures intended to throw light on the progress of a passion. Only the proportions are different.

In this way, Zaïde is in some respects the mirror image of La Princesse de Clèves. The first flashback of Zaïde, Consalve's deception by Nugna Bella, is quite parallel to the second digression of La Princesse de Clèves, the Mme de Tournon episode, in that both relate the duplicity of a mistress and her betrayal of a reproachless lover. And the second flashback of Zaïde, Alphonse's irrational jealousy of Bélasire (who figuratively dies to the world by taking the veil), is in turn related to the third digression of La Princesse de Clèves, in which Henry VIII's unfounded jealousy leads to Anne Boleyn's ruin and death.

Part II of Zaïde begins with Consalve's return to Leon, where he finds his sister, contrary to his expectations, married to Don Garcie. The Prince apologizes for his conduct, saying "I only failed [your friendship] because of a passion that takes the wits away from those it seizes" (136). The inevitable flashback then follows (much shorter this time), the "Story of Don Garcie and Hermenesilde." Consalve learns that Don Ramire and Nugna Bella have both received their harsh deserts: the former has conveniently perished in battle, and the latter, repenting her past infidelities, has been married by her father to a German bigot of unpleasant character.

War with the Moors breaks out, and Don Garcie makes Consalve his general. Upon capturing the castle of Talavera, Consalve is surprised to find Zaïde, who, it turns out, is the daughter of Zuléma, commander of the Moorish forces. The two lovers approach each other, Consalve speaking Greek, and Zaïde Spanish. The cloying charm of this highly *romanesque* scene might metaphorically signal the military-amorous "conquest" of Zaïde, but new obstacles immediately arise. Zaïde's evasiveness in explaining her tears at Tarragon leads Consalve to suspect that she really loves Alamir, Prince of Tharsis, a Saracen warrior who is passionately in love with her, and who accompanied her on the ill-fated voyage from Cyprus. Consalve happens to wound and capture Alamir in single combat; he gallantly saves his rival's life, but his troops demand Alamir's execution in retribution for atrocities committed by the Moors. At the same time, Félime intervenes to beg Consalve to spare Alamir. Consalve has no doubt that Félime is only acting for Zaïde, but accedes to her request on condition that she explain their interest in Alamir. The action, properly speaking, of *Zaïde* is terminated. Except for the final dénouement (marriage), the remainder of *Zaïde* is consumed in a series of three lengthy flashbacks.

In the first of these, the "Story of Zaïde and Félime," we learn that the two women are cousins from Cyprus. Although their fathers are Arabs, they themselves are Christians (thus another potential barrier, difference of religion, is removed, making Zaïde's comportment toward Consalve all the more puzzling). Alamir falls in love with Zaïde, who rebuffs him, and Félime falls in love with Alamir, who hardly notices her. This "story" is narrated by Félime, whose curiosity about the man she loves leads her to ask his companion to tell the "Story of Alamir, Prince of Tharsis."

IV *Alamir*

No other character in Mme de Lafayette so clearly prefigures Nemours (and to some extent, M. de Clèves), Mme de Clèves' suitor, as does Alamir. The Don Juan psychology, only briefly hinted at in *La Princesse de Montpensier,* is fully developed in the person of Alamir the fickle, *le volage.* In fact Alamir's career is Nemours' past; his exploits are those which public rumor attributes to Nemours (and which the reader takes on faith), who was "so disposed to gallantry that he could not refuse some attentions to the women who tried to please him; so he had several loves, but it was difficult to guess which lady he truly loved" (244). Alamir's adventures, unlike Nemours', are detailed for us, and like Guise, Alphonse, Don Ramire, and Nemours, he clearly relishes the prospect of obstacles to overcome: "He sought only the pleasure of being loved; that of loving was unknown to him. . . . As soon as he was loved, as he had nothing more to desire and was not enough in love to find pleasure in love alone . . . he only thought of breaking off with the woman he had loved in order to make another love him" (175).[8]

Alamir is equally adept at juggling several affairs at once. Struck by Naria's beauty, virtue, and riches, he tries assiduously to court her, at the same time as he showers his attentions on Zoromade. Arab mores, which condone polygamy and strictly regulate women's conduct and restrain their independence, are exactly suited to Alamir's temperament, for he thrives on both the multiplicity of his loves and the barriers he must surmount. The difficulties of seeing Zoromade are even greater than those of seeing Naria, but Alamir is not so anxious to "overcome these obstacles as Naria's resistance, which came from her alone." Alamir is a conqueror in love. But when Naria unexpectedly provides him with a secret rendezvous of her own devising and forthrightly avows her "inclination" for Alamir, he is robbed of the delights of conquest: "as there were no more obstacles or difficulties in seeing her, his love began to diminish"; and thus he turns again to Zoromade: "the impossibility of seeing her was still the same, and so his passion was even greater." Alamir cleverly succeeds in winning her love, but his unfaithfulness is soon found out, and Naria, humiliated and ashamed, writes him an accusing letter.

Alamir's companion severely reproaches him for his faithless and dishonorable conduct, but Alamir, who is more than a lecherous skirt-chaser, retorts that the constancy of his love depends upon a separation of his person and his position: "Naria thought she loved me; but she loved my rank, to which I could elevate her. I have found only vanity and ambition in all women: they loved the prince and not Alamir. . . . You'd see that I would not be incapable of faithful love, if I could find a person who loved me without knowing who I am" (181). As always in Mme de Lafayette, all reasoning about future love, all speculations on future conduct (especially those premised on past experience) are abstract and crumble in the face of passion experienced in the present. If morality is a code, a projection meant to govern eventuality, then love is its own morality; it answers to no standards pre-existing to the ones it discovers or invents for itself.

The narrative provides Alamir with a test of this personal "truth" he has just posited, for he is soon infatuated with Elsibery, the daughter of the governor of Lemnos, and thus someone who does not recognize Alamir as the Prince of Tharsis. It would be tedious to recount the numerous tests to which Alamir subjects Elsibery's love for him.[9] It is enough to say that her love survives the cruellest trials: "She loved him with no other intention than loving him, and without asking the end her passion would have; she did not inform herself of his fortune or his intentions; she took great risks to see him and blindly did everything he could ask for" (192). When Elsibery at last learns Alamir's true identity, she is filled with joy to know that her lover is also a prince. All Alamir's subterfuges now become precious to her as proofs of his sincerity, and her passion redoubles. But for Alamir, this increase is suspect. Had he then not known the *full* measure of her love, and was her renewed ardor directed, not to him, but to the Prince? Inevitably his love begins to secrete its own poison; insensibly his love wanes and he plans a voyage to Cyprus to get away from Elsibery.

Was this love? Apparently not, for until he falls in love with Zaïde on Cyprus, he had never hesitated to state his passions quite forwardly, whereas with Zaïde he becomes shy and reticent. Moreover, there is no mention in the text of jealousy until Alamir sees Consalve as a potential rival for Zaïde's hand, and most important, Zaïde is indifferent to his declarations. For Alamir, and for every Don Juan, love and will are synonymous in that they imply an equation between self-mastery, action, and conquest, whence the rout and confusion of this Don Juan, disarmed by indifference:

What! The only *power* love ever had over me was what I *wished* to allow it; and now, through the only person in the world in whom I have found *resistance,* it *dominates* me with an *empire* so absolute that I have no *power* left to free myself. I was incapable of loving all those who loved me. Zaïde scorns me and I adore her. Is it her wonderful beauty that produces such an exceptional effect? or is it possible that the only way to hold me is not to love me? (199; my italics)

Here is Alamir's real truth: it is not to be loved only for himself, but simply not to be loved. He loves as long as love is an impossibility, or as long as it remains unrealized. (This is exactly what Mme de Clèves suspects of Nemours: "I even believe that the obstacles have made you constant." [387]). Alamir is a new Tantalus, who can bless the receding waters for his thirst, for satiety would bring dissatisfaction; paradoxically, he must be thankful for his jealousy, which is his happiness.

The narrative returns to the "Continuation of the Story of Félime and Zaïde," the last flashback, and we encounter the last obstacle in the path of Zaïde and Consalve's love. This is a matter of a small portrait that Zaïde found one day in Zuléma's affairs. It appears to be the portrait of an Arab prince, and it so strikes Zaïde's fancy that her father's astrologer jokingly predicts that she will marry the man in the portrait. Zuléma unaccountably takes the prediction seriously and ·vows that his daughter will never marry any other man. The shipwreck that stranded Zaïde and Félime in Tarragon then ensues, and the ladies' fascination with the puzzling resemblance between the "Arab" of the portrait and the Spaniard Consalve. Zaïde falls in love with Consalve, but stubbornly remains faithful to her "duty" to wed the unknown man of the portrait.

After some highly *précieux* resistance on the part of Zaïde and the death of Alamir from his wounds (and Félime of unrequited love for him), we learn that the portrait that fell into Zuléma's hands did so at his defeat of Nugnez Fernando, Consalve's father. Zuléma explains that he only insisted that Zaïde marry the man of the portrait because he looked very much like the Prince of Fez, to whom he intended to wed his daughter. Zuléma further announces his intention to be converted to the Christian religion and gives his blessing to the union of Zaïde and Consalve, which is celebrated "with all the gallantry of the Moors and the civility of Spain."

All in all, *Zaïde*, despite some of the engrossing psychologies of love that it presents, is an unsatisfying exercise. Its style is precious, its events improbable, the lovers' obstacles are wholly outward, and its characters are overreflective and melancholy. This would not be in itself detrimental were the narrative not so mired in explanations and analysis that it founders under its own intellectual weight. *Zaïde* is fundamentally the demonstration of a premise, that true passion is immediate—a *coup de foudre*—rather than the result of knowledge. Nevertheless it shows how problems of self-knowledge and self-mastery "become acute in the presence of strong passions";[10] it marks continuity from Mme de Lafayette's first novel; and it adumbrates modalities of *La Princesse de Clèves*, or at least the tenor of her masterpiece.

CHAPTER 5

La Princesse de Clèves

I Questions and Objections

Regularity and harmony are commonly cited as characteristics of French Classicism. It is therefore curious to observe that, whereas *La Princesse de Clèves* is hailed as the prototype of the aerodynamic and unilinear *récit* that supposedly is peculiarly French and Classical, it is just as often criticized for its irregularities and imbalances. Immediately following the publication of the novel the famous digressions, for example, were attacked as superfluous and as detracting from the unity of the work. In his countercritique, the Abbé de Charnes, although taking some pains to justify these episodes, dismissed the question as trivial and blandly asserted that "it is not necessary to link [episodes] to the main subject of a work; it suffices to tie them to the particular place where they are introduced."[1]

Still another difficulty of the book, whose precise nature is more delicate to frame, is its tonality, which becomes still more perplexing when one considers that no reader is insensitive to certain stylistic quirks that are vexingly at odds with our preconceived notions of what French Classical prose is. In what other seventeenth-century writers of Mme de Lafayette's reputation must we contend with such labyrinthine and Latinate scatterings of *qui* and *que,* such vague use of pronouns, such ritual repetitiveness of narrative formulas like "he said" and "she said"? Nor can we easily neglect the paucity of a vocabulary that is abstract and general to the point of vagueness. In effect, what distinctions are implied or intended among such complementary terms as *attachement, commerce, engagement, galanterie, inclination, liaison?*

Why is there at once an impression of profusion and compression in this novel? If, according to Segrais, Mme de Lafayette really claimed that "to strike a period out of a work was worth a *louis d'or,* and a word twenty *sols,*"[2] why could not she have done some judicious pruning? On the other hand, why must a blush or a silence bear so much significance in a work that is ostensibly devoted to minute psychological investigation? And with such a complexity of motives offered as explanations for the Princess' final renunciation, why do we still remain on the tonal periphery of her decision? All these questions are raised by a reading of *La Princesse de Clèves.*

To many of these question there are no answers, or rather one can answer that Mme de Lafayette did not possess the stylistic mastery that her novel's reputation has led us to expect. This is not to say, however, that the book lacks organization or that its meaning is obscured by an apparently chaotic structure. On the contrary, *La Princesse de Clèves* has great unity, and its meaning derives directly from its form.

Let us begin with questions of form, and with Mme de Lafayette's contention that the novel was really *memoirs* in which one sees "a perfect imitation of the court and its ways" (C II, 63). The sentence seems to promise a richness of portrayal that is inconsistent with the sense of monotony—in the sense of a single tone—that we gain from *La Princesse de Clèves.* Albert Camus found in its "passionate monotony" the very cachet of its Classical foundations, and wrote: "To be Classical is to repeat oneself. Thus we find, in the heart of our greatest novelistic works, a certain conception of man that intelligence strives to represent by means of a small number of situations."[3] Camus' remark is perceptive and sums up the reader's impression of the tone of *La Princesse de Clèves.* But the task of explaining this monotony within the context of Mme de Lafayette's own remark, which strongly implies diversity, still remains. To frame the question in another way, how many worlds are there really in this novel? There seem to be two, the relatively circumscribed world of the Princess, and the larger one of the court. From a modern perspective, these worlds could be contrasted as subjective and objective, personal and historical, and so on. We attach no value judgments to these terms, but we should remember that Mme de Lafayette's contemporaries did and that they considered that the personal and subjective worlds were imaginary and synonymous with all that is fantastic and *unreal*. To impose that unreal world as the only convincingly authentic one of the novel would constitute a great tour de force, and this is exactly what Mme de Lafayette has succeeded in doing. She has succeeded in leading the reader from history to fiction all the while persuading him, paradoxically, that his progress is progress toward "real" reality, the authenticity of an *expérience vécue*.

II *The Outside and the Inside of* La Princesse de Clèves

Camus' remark on "monotony" is suggestive, for it directs the reader's attention to an obvious stylistic feature of the novel, the predominant use of the imperfect tense. The imperfect is clearly utilized to the "monotonous" end of which Camus spoke, for in French, the imperfect tense has the effect of stripping the narrative of its immediacy precisely through the suggestion of habit or repetition. This has immediate consequences on the "outward" world of *La Princesse de Clèves*, for this world, which is essentially the parade and spectacle of the court, is robbed of its turgid quality. It no longer stands out in relief from the context, but is forced to remain on the same plane, and indeed to compete for the reader's attention with the *récit intérieur*, or inner story, of the heroine. It will progressively give way to this *récit* and will eventually be subsumed in it. In short, the imperfect tense is one of several stylistic features that makes outward events, "history" if we like, seem superficial and ultimately unreal. This movement, from the outside to the inside, is the reader's itinerary, and its way is clearly blazed. Its start is in the opening sentence "Splendor and gallantry have never appeared in France with such brilliance as during the last years of the reign of Henri II," and its finish in Mme de Chartres' admonitory remark, "If you judge by appearances in this place, you will often be deceived; what appears is almost never the truth" (265).

Thus the reader's attention is constantly directed toward the inner story, through indirect discourse (and in some instances an astonishing pre-Flaubertian *style indirect libre*) and interior monologue wherein the heroine's innermost reflections are revealed.[4] In this way, thoughts really become the substance of the action, and analysis supersedes event. This internalization constitutes nothing less than a reversal of the proportions of the *roman romanesque*; it marks an enormous progress over *Zaïde*, where actions are explained by a ritual return to the past (the flashback) rather than by an interior monologue that discloses, simultaneously with the event, its unsettling significance. That private meaning is meditative by nature and not even the dialogues can temper its rigidly somber register.

There is little vivacity or naturalness to Mme de Lafayette's dialogues if by these words we designate a representational means of reproducing the spoken word. French has never used quotation marks in the same way English does to make a conversation stand out from the text. (Indeed, the use of *tirets* or dashes to indicate direct discourse is largely an eighteenth-century invention.) Mme de Lafayette's only indication that we have moved from indirect to direct quotation is a formulaic "he said" or "she replied," stylistic transitions that scarcely evoke a flicker of recognition from the reader. All this might be viewed unfavorably, but there is much to be said in support of Jean Fabre's contention that we must understand the dearth of narrative invention and virtuosity as a function of the book's overall register, instead of finding evidence of a retarded or rudimentary technique. The style, he says, is a *style pensé* and not a *style parlé*; consequently attempts to evaluate the novel in terms of spoken style result in an esthetic contretemps that misjudges the ceremonial quality of the book.[5]

A "lively" dialogue, also meant to convey a "sense of life," would detract from the meditative and even ethical mood of the novel. Esthetically it would make no sense, for it would constitute the counterpart of the "splendor and gallantry" away from which the reader steadily moves. Thus we may conclude that the style of *La Princesse de Clèves* is *untextured,* that the compression of the narrative creates a deliberate sensation of distance in the reader: as well as "conniving" (in the interior monologues) he continues to observe with objectivity. Knowledge does not entail familiarity, and *tout comprendre* is not *tout pardonner.*

The inwardness of *La Princesse de Clèves* is accomplished in many ways and is Mme de Lafayette's finest achievement. She has made obliqueness the secret weave of her novel, in both form and content. We shall shortly see how this obliqueness functions thematically and how it leads to moral ambiguousness in our judgment of the heroine.

If the style of the novel is deliberately untextured, the historical underpinnings are just as consciously articulated to insure the passage from without to within. In Chapter 2, it was seen that the use of history was envisaged by several writers as a means of infusing truth into fictional creations, either by simple juxtaposition or by more astute interpenetration. This is to a large extent true of *La Princesse de Montpensier*. The relationship is a good deal subtler in *La Princesse de Clèves* and is best understood by grasping the implications of Mme de Chartres' previously quoted remark on truth and appearance: judging outward forms is conducive to error, for appearance is a mask. (Mme de Chartres had just explained to her daughter the complexities of Diane de Poitiers' liaison with Henri II.) This is only the first step in the Princess' instruction in the ways of the court, but already it sets the tone for the subsequent revelations, the core of which is that in a court whose soul is dissimulation, the "inside" story is the only true story. This is true of all the digressions: Diane de Poitiers is apparently faithful to the King, but he is openly jealous of the Comte de Brissac and also has "other reasons" to be jealous; Mme de Tournon's doubletiming was outwardly the strictest faithfulness; Henry VIII's jealousy was really lust for another woman; the Vidame's love affairs, far from elevating him as he hoped, will eventually lead to his disgrace and death. The suggestion that nearly all court relationships are a façade, and that truth and reality reside somewhere within, strengthens the reader's sense of the artificiality of the purely historical episodes. Mistrust of the outer trappings inevitably leads to the assumption that the secrets of the heart are the only hard reality, and in this manner, the more the book becomes fictional (Mme de Clèves' awakening interest in the Duc de Nemours) the more it becomes real. In one sense this corresponds to one of the commonplaces of the Classical esthetic, the preference for the *vraisemblable* over the *vrai*. But in another, more profound sense, it is evidence that Mme de Lafayette has resolved, in an original way, the vexing question of the proportions and relationship of history and fiction that so preoccupied writers and critics of the *nouvelle historique*. As Jean Rousset writes, "Far from it being history that guarantees fiction, as the theory had it, here the imaginary world triumphs with all the fascination of reality, and relegates historical reality to the role of futile decor and meaningless records."[6]

This also explains, to some degree, the nature of the digressions, which are confined to the first half of the novel. They cannot merely be external local color, for if this were the case, why should there not be more of them? The answer is of course that they are intended for the Princess' instruction. From the reader's viewpoint, they form an important part of her education and function like a prelude to the Princess' story.[7] Indeed, the interventions of history or of external points of reference are absent from the last half of the novel: the Princess' own drama invades our field of vision with an intensity that history can never rival. The substitution of fiction's reality for that of fact is the sign of all great novels, and in Mme de Lafayette's time it was an artistic feat of the first magnitude.

III   The Digressions

The digressions have drawn much critical attention in modern times. (In the seventeenth century the confession elicited the most criticism; this may be indicative of our own questionable preoccupation with form over content.) Yet once some cumbersome and ungainly defects are conceded, they remain functionally unambiguous, for they provide the objective initiation that leads into the Princess' own experience of love. Moreover, they are digressions only in the sense that action is momentarily suspended; they remain relevant in that they are thematically linked to the main plot.

For memory's sake, let us recall that they are four in number, and that their principals are respectively Diane de Poitiers (Mme de Valentinois), Mme de Tournon, Anne Boleyn, and the Vidame de Chartres. All four stories are naturally love stories, and all involve duplicity. There are successful and unsuccessful intrigues, and in the case of the former, there are examples of women—Diane de Poitiers and Mme de Tournon —who cleverly deceive two men at the same time. Further, they are progressively modulated to mesh with the Princess' own awakening.

La Princesse de Cleves

The first episode—Diane de Poitiers' liaison with Henri II—is historically and morally remote from the innocence of the young girl to whom her mother relates the tale. It is, from Mlle de Chartres' standpoint, merely an illustration of the statement, historically phrased (i.e. from without) that "ambition and gallantry were the soul of the court" (252), or an explication of the same court's dangerous and alluring "agitation without disorder" (253).

The next episode—Sancerre's discovery after Mme de Tournon's death of her infidelity—told to Mme de Clèves by her husband, narrows the distance between history and heroine, otherwise, between the "other" and the "self." It becomes embarrassingly tangential. M. de Clèves is recounting the advice he offered his friend Sancerre:

"I am giving you," said I, "the same advice I would take myself, for sincerity so appeals to me that I think that if my mistress, or even my wife, confessed to me that she was attracted by someone, I would be grieved without being embittered. I would drop the role of lover or husband, to advise and pity her."
These words made Mme de Clèves blush, for she found they had a certain application to her own state that surprised her and caused an uneasiness from which she was some time in recovering. (284)

The third digression (the *reine dauphine*'s account of the life of Anne Boleyn), weakly and erroneously justified by the Abbé de Charnes as central to the Princess' interest in "a Queen who was such a dangerous rival," [8] seems the least apposite, although it does fit into the pattern of protection—mother, husband, patroness (for Mme de Clèves is a "favorite" of the Dauphiness)—that unites the narrators in their relationship to the Princess. Like M. de Clèves, moreover, Mary Stuart tells a proleptic story: it announces her fate, for like the subject of her narrative, Anne Boleyn, she too will be beheaded. More importantly, this "digression" personalizes the events of the novel, which, with the final episode, evolve from the anecdotal and irrelevant to the unconsciously, and at last consciously, pertinent.

The most important feature of the fourth episode (in which the Princess reads a letter addressed to the Vidame de Chartres which she mistakenly supposes to have been addressed to

Nemours) is that if the letter is not addressed to the heroine, it is read by her, and comes from a woman (Mme de Thémines) who has been deceived by her lover and who breaks off with him.[9] Thus, in relation to the previous episodes, the letter assumes an even more direct relevance: it becomes personalized history. This articulation clearly marks the passage from the objective to the subjective. None of the Princess' protectors—or screens, as they may be called—tells her this story. She has changed from witness to actor. She has alarmingly bridged the reassuring gap that seemed to guarantee her moral safety, to separate "virtue" from "gallantry." And when she symbolically takes a hand in composing the substitute letter designed to deceive the Queen, she has moved far from her initial innocence to the sacred egotism of love and its frightening repercussions:

M. de Nemours was very glad to prolong an interview that was so pleasant and forgot his friend's interests. Mme de Clèves was not bored herself and also forgot the interests of her uncle. At last the letter was barely finished by four o'clock, and so badly done, and the handwriting of the copy so little resembled the hand they intended to imitate, that the Queen would have had not to try at all not to find out the truth. So she was not deceived by it, in spite of the efforts made to persuade her that the letter was addressed to M. de Nemours. She remained convinced, not only that it was to the Vidame de Chartres, but also that the Dauphiness had some part in it, and that there was an understanding between them. This thought so intensified her hatred of this princess that she never forgave her, and she persecuted her until she had made her leave France. As for the Vidame, he was ruined with her. (328–29)

Thus, far from digressing, the final digression leads the reader *inside* the novel to the true scene of action, and Mme de Clèves to the troubled mirror of her conscience. Reader and character, the screens removed, gaze upon the harsh realities of passion: mistrust, jealousy, guilt, shame; in sum, a moral and rational impotence that also includes awareness. The Princess awakens— "She awakened as from a dream"—her eyes are unsealed:

Although the suspicions [of Nemours' infidelity] that the letter had given her were dispelled, they did not fail to open her eyes to the chance of being deceived and to give her feelings of mistrust and jealousy that she had never entertained. She was astonished that she had not thought sooner how unlikely it was that a man like M. de Nemours, who had always treated women so lightly, should be capable of a sincere and lasting relationship. She found it nearly impossible to be satisfied with his love. "And if I could be," she said, "what would I do with it? Do I mean to tolerate it? Do I mean to respond to it? Do I mean to embark upon a love affair? Do I mean to fail M. de Clèves? Do I mean to fail myself? And finally, do I mean to expose myself to the cruel repentance and deadly anguish that come from love? I am defeated and overcome by an inclination that sweeps me away in spite of myself. All my resolutions are unavailing. . . ." (330)

Resolute action, she feels, is incumbent on her, even if its only outcome is to help her regain self-possession. The thought of revealing her inclination for Nemours to her husband has previously crossed her mind. She now thinks that to achieve peace of mind she may be forced to instruct M. de Clèves of her dangerous penchant: "I must go to the country, however strange my departure may seem; and if M. de Clèves insists on stopping me or on knowing my reasons, perhaps I shall hurt him, and myself too, by telling them to him" (330–31).

We can perceive in this resolution an act of courage, if we like, and in the confession scene, the heroine herself presents it in such a light. But the Princess' confession lets us glimpse more than a hint of abandon when we place it within the overall pattern that winds throughout the book, the screen motif that was earlier mentioned, a kind of schema of moral interposition that is intimately linked to the style and structure of *La Princesse de Clèves*. For this novel may be accurately described, in all its modalities, as a study of obliqueness and opacity.

IV Screens

Returning to Mme de Chartres and the period of her daughter's education, we note that the very first principle to which she directs the young girl's attention is virtue. Virtue is, for Mme de Chartres, essentially a defense mechanism, guarding against "men's insincerity, their deceit and faithlessness" and is practiced negatively, by *"an extreme mistrust of oneself"* (248). The extent to which this mistrust is conducive to lack of confidence in oneself is problematic, but the very existence of virtue presupposes a standard of conduct, exterior and concrete, a point of reference that, *faute de mieux,* is incarnated for Mlle de Chartres in the most accessible figure of authority: her mother. This is all the more natural in that Mme de Chartres, if authoritative in this sense, is not authoritarian. She is very much the modern mother, begging her daughter, "not as her mother, but as her friend, to confide in her all the gallant things that would be said to her, and promising to help guide her in matters in which a young person is often embarrassed" (253). Unfortunately, Mme de Chartres has no modern scruples about giving her daughter in marriage to a man for whom she only professes "less repugnance than for another" (258).

Mme de Clèves accepts her mother's offer, and when the Chevalier de Guise, whose hopes of marriage with Mlle de Chartres were cut short for reasons of family prestige and politics, continues to pay court to her, she confides to her mother that her pity for him "did not lead to other feelings; she told her mother the sorrow that this prince's affection caused her" (259). The mother responds to her daughter's "sincerity," but knowing that M. de Clèves has not touched her heart any more than has Guise, she fortifies the Princess' sense of duty to her husband and "joined to her daughter's decorum such precise observation of social conventions that she completed her appearance as a person of unassailable reputation" (260).

So does virtue become the distance separating an outward appearance and an indeterminate inward being. And so the habit of confession as an exercise in virtue is ingrained in the Princess. The ball scene, to which we now turn, will shatter these fragile arrangements.

The Dauphiness has already spoken admiringly of the Duc de Nemours, and the Princess is both curious and impatient to see him.

The ball opened, and while she was dancing with M. de Guise, there was a great stir at the door as if someone was entering for whom people were making way. Mme de Clèves finished the dance, and while her eyes sought someone whom she meant to take as a partner, the King called out to her to take the newcomer. She turned and saw a man who she thought at once could be no other than M. de Nemours, stepping over some seats to reach the dancing floor.

This prince was such that it was difficult not to be surprised upon seeing him for the first time . . . but it was equally difficult to see Mme de Clèves for the first time without astonishment. . . . When they began to dance, a murmur of praise arose in the room. The King and Queen recalled that they had never met, and found something singular in their dancing together without knowing each other. (261–62)

The social identities of the couple—Nemours the glorious suitor of Queens, and the Princesse de Clèves, the blonde beauty of the court—seem to dissolve in their mutual surprise, a term toward whose significance the reader of Zaïde is fully keyed. This is a match, both as a union and as a contest, whose first steps take place in full view of the court, the arena, so to speak, of their confrontation. To reach the Princess, Nemours must negotiate some mildly symbolic obstacles, and the Princess must fulfill the command of her sovereign, whose voice, calling out for her to take Nemours, assumes all the coercion of destiny: *vox regis, vox dei.*[10]

Their "surprise," which grows in the following days, does not escape the jealous eye of Guise (the courtier's favorite pasttime is not the theater for nothing) nor the watchfulness of Mme de Chartres. Its meaning escapes only the protagonist herself, who naively babbles of Nemours' great merits to her mother.

This innocence, which is really inability to perceive (before it becomes refusal to perceive), is again related to the motif of obliqueness. It is notable that the first digression, playing on the theme of fidelity and infidelity through Diane de Poitiers' story, is introduced immediately after this episode. Its location helps to define the general nature of the episodes, which is, in the absence of the Princess' ability to see herself, to provide an exterior crystallization of consciousness. It is more than a portion of her sentimental education.

The Princess never really "catches up" with herself. Unlike the others—Mme de Chartres, her husband, Guise, Nemours—she cannot see herself acting, and her involuntary or spontaneous acts, which others interpret on the spot, precede reflection and *deliver* her, morally naked, to the world. This will provoke bewilderment and fear in her. It generates a fear of spontaneity, even of genuineness, that she masks in various ways (duty, reason, etc.) knowing ultimately that these are artifices. The heroine cannot see herself and so seeks or finds (it is really the same) clarification from the outside. (To return parenthetically to matters of style, this explains the use of the third-person narrative in *La Princesse de Clèves* and makes it something more than the reflexive imitation of a seventeenth century narrative convention.)

The birth of love engenders deception in the Princess, and she begins unconsciously, following the habit of the court, to dissimulate:

> She did not feel as inclined to tell her mother what she thought of [Nemours'] sentiments as she did with her other suitors; without deliberately hiding the matter, she did not mention it to her mother. But Mme de Chartres saw this only too well, in addition to the penchant that her daughter had for him. (270)

When Mme de Chartres, as a warning to her daughter, suggests that Nemours is really interested in the Dauphiness, the Princess is astonished and wonders if she is not serving as a decoy for Nemours' suit of this lady. She also consciously knows for the first time (but apparently without knowing that jealousy sharpens her insight) that she is in love with Nemours and so determines to tell her mother all. But the next morning her mother is taken by fever, and her confession must be remanded.

The fever turns into a serious illness, and after a few days, Mme de Chartres summons her daughter to her bedside to give her last advice and farewell. This muted scene, one of the most moving in *La Princesse de Clèves*, portrays Mme de Chartres stoically resigned to death and finding strength to warn her daughter against gallantry. For she knows that Mme de Clèves is enamoured of Nemours and urges her to muster all her virtue and sense of duty to resist: "do not fear to take very harsh and difficult measures; however terrible they may appear at first, in the end they will be gentler than the evils of an affair." The Princess can only weep silently during this scene, until her mother tenderly and resolutely dismisses her: "Farewell, my daughter, let us end a conversation that moves us both too deeply, and remember, if you can, all I have just told you" (278).

Mme de Chartres lives on for two more days, but refuses to see her daughter—"the only person she held dear." When she dies, the Princess knows that she has lost a protector, and a certain rebalancing of spiritual weights must ensue.

We can easily surmise that the circumstances of her mother's death have a profound effect upon the Princess. The coincidence of her nascent love for Nemours and her mother's illness and death is of course fortuitous, but the acute remorse of having her mother guess something that the usually confiding daughter had not thought fit to tell her must surely engender, even amorphously, feelings of guilt. In the full sense of the phrase, the Princess has *quelque chose sur le cœur*.

At this point the second digression intervenes, the Mme de Tournon episode in which M. de Clèves says "I think that if my mistress, or even my wife, confessed to me that she was attracted by someone, I would be grieved without being embittered" (284). It is easy to see how skillfully Mme de Lafayette is preparing the confession scene by effecting a transfer of the Princess' reliance on authority from the dead mother to the living husband. Coincidentally, there evolves a terrifying separation between the Princess' public person and her private being: "She was about to tell him that a rumor was abroad of M. de Nemours being in love with her; but she did not have the strength to name him. She also felt ashamed at wishing to use a false reason and to hide the truth from a man who had such a high opinion of her" (296).

The daily routine of visits, of attending court, has become torture for the Princess, who can barely perform, so distracted is she by the disparity between her appearance and her reality. By this time the very phrase "to appear in society" alludes to a whole line of conduct bordered with pitfalls dug by the exigencies of the seeming presence, that is, the exterior she must maintain. When Nemours surreptitiously makes off with her portrait, unobserved by any but her (and she is secretly "happy to grant him a favor in her power without his even being aware of it"), her distress is acute, because the portrait—her image—assumes a nearly talismanic significance. It seems that the last garland of her moral façade has been plucked away, leaving her defenseless: "there was nothing left to defend her" (303).

Remembering her husband's opinion of sincerity, she determines to tell him of her inclination; then she immediately rejects this course of action as "folly." She finds that she is no longer "mistress of her words or feelings" (twice repeated in the text) and until the confession scene itself, we know that she is only postponing the choice between two sorts of folly.

There is a false interlude to her dilemma. Prior to the episode of Mme de Thémines' letter, every exchange between the Princess and Nemours has been typically muted: a blush, a glance, a discreet compliment are limits that have not been transgressed. The letter provides a fleeting and single instance of joyous and innocent intimacy. Moreover, it is sanctioned by the unobtrusive presence of M. de Clèves and the thought of a task to be performed. It therefore passes under the guise of a community of interests. (It is true that M. de Clèves leaves the lovers together for an instant of privacy which allows Nemours to dispel the Princess' suspicions that the letter was addressed to him—"one is easily convinced of an agreeable truth"—but this scene, like the final interview, is really a confrontation, in the sense of an attack and defense of tangled personal motives.)

They resolved to rewrite the letter from memory. They shut themselves up to work on it, gave orders that no one was to enter, and dismissed all M. de Nemours' servants. This atmosphere of mystery and confidence was not mediocrely charming for the Duke and even for Mme de Clèves. The presence of her husband and the interests of her uncle reassured her scruples somewhat. She felt only the pleasure of seeing M. de Nemours, and this gave her a pure and unmixed joy that she had never experienced. This joy gave her an ease and playfulness of spirit that M. de Nemours had never seen in her before, and which increased his love twofold. (328)

Here is the only place in the novel where the Princess is not gripped by the tensions of her virtue, where the background, with its garish festoons of appearance, constraint, and guilt no longer projects its shadow over her conscience. Inevitably she comes to view it as a lapse, a moment of forgetfulness and unreason. This brief moment in which her moral and public selves coincide, obliterating that reassuring chasm which she names virtue, engenders the violent reaction that leads to the confession. The glaring juxtaposition of her initial coldness toward Nemours and her subsequent happiness at being convinced that he had nothing to do with the letter is only one inconsistency in her conduct that she finds intolerable. How to reestablish, indeed, to widen that distance that preserves what she now begins to call her *repos*? How to repair the disruptions of passion, to attain coherence anew? For the Princess aspires to coherence, not to the distinction of true from false. If stability cannot be achieved from the inside, then it must be sought from without, from a screen. And her husband, her master, represents the only appeal, the only accession to order through authority. Her mother has already made the pattern familiar to her, and confession, now as then, she imagines, is the proof and result of sincerity. The Princess' lucid existence has become a dull transparency, as if the lamp that lighted it had been snuffed out. She seeks illumination, and it is here that the boundaries between morality and expediency become fluid, if not viscous.

V   The Confession

The Princess is not so naive as to suppose that confession of her love for Nemours will not profundly disturb her husband, but this is not the question that the modern reader asks. It is rather, would a wife who genuinely cares for her husband's wellbeing admit such a situation to him? And to this particular husband, who has always suffered intensely, as his wife well knows, from the knowledge that his wife has never truly responded to his love, but only to his merits? "He always had something to wish for beyond possessing her, and although she lived on perfect terms with him, he was not entirely happy" (260). One of La Rochefoucauld's maxims seems very appropriate here: "We are sometimes less unhappy being deceived by the ones we love, than being undeceived" (Maxim 395). And speaking of Mme de Clèves' literary contemporaries, can we not prefer the bourgeois practicality of Molière's Elmire? Her situation is altogether different in that the repulsive Tartuffe has little in common with the seductive Nemours, but Elmire's commonsensical words do seem to apply:

> Ce n'est point mon humeur de faire des éclats:
> Une femme se rit de sottises pareilles,
> Et jamais d'un mari n'en trouble les oreilles.[11]

This aspect of the problem is exactly the one that interested Mme de Lafayette's first readers, or at least those who expressed their opinions of the confession to the *Mercure Galant.* They did not understand or care about the psychological and literary function of the confession. They did not question the Princess' sincerity; rather they criticized her action for its social consequences: it was disruptive of marriage, and so forth.

Today our use of ethical terms is generally relative. When we utter such words—virtue, for example—we no longer hear them as irreducibles, as expressing qualities of one piece, whole and wholesome. Just as we no longer believe that the atom is an irreducible structure, we no longer believe that sincerity (or any virtue, for that matter) is an ethical unity that can be left unexamined. Mme de Clèves' motives seem suspect to us, then. Does Mme de Lafayette see the insincerity of her heroine's conduct? She maintains her objectivity, letting the reader decide. Her viewpoint, however, is only esthetically oblique, which is not the same as the character's imperception.

There is no reason to assume that Mme de Lafayette is unaware of the darker side of Mme de Clèves' pristine frankness. She indirectly suggests as much by the tone of smugness and formalistic remorse that creeps into the Princess' *aveu.* There is a great deal of confession here, but little contrition. Mme de Clèves' words bear much more on the continuation of outward appearances than on any projected repentance and reform: "I have never given the least sign of weakness and I would not fear giving any if you gave me the liberty of withdrawing from the court or if I still had Mme de Chartres to help guide me. . . . I beg your pardon earnestly if I have feelings that grieve you; at least I will never grieve you by my actions" (333–34).

Mme de Clèves' confession tells both too much and too little; its greatest danger is that it opens vistas on unsuspected and forbidden regions which her husband's mind can never explore to satisfaction. The situation is Alphonse and Bélasire all over again. M. de Clèves' immediate speculation is of course the name of his wife's suitor; it draws this response:

"You would insist in vain. I have strength enough not to reveal what I think I ought not to. My confession to you was not from weakness, and it requires more courage to admit this truth than to undertake to hide it. . . ." M. de Clèves was nevertheless doing all he could to find out the name, and after he had pressed her for it in vain, she replied: "It seems to me that you should be satisfied with my sincerity; do not ask me for more, and do not give me cause to regret what I have just done. Be satisfied with the further assurance that no action of mine has made my feelings apparent, and that nothing has ever been said to me at which I might take offense." (335)

There is something cavalier and condescending, even odious, in these words. Moreover, there is a curious reversal in the respective positions of M. and Mme de Clèves that is reminiscent of the Princesse de Montpensier's egotistic confidences to Chabanes. By the end of the scene, it is the Princess who is remonstrative, and the offended party, the Prince, who is apologetic and nearly self-reproachful: " 'You are right, madam,' he said, 'I am unfair. Refuse to answer whenever I ask you such things; but do not take offense if I ask them' " (336).

Once launched upon her perilous confession, the Princess acquires a self-mastery and confidence that are at odds with her initial misgivings. The configuration, the "singularity" of her *aveu* disturbs her more than its content, and she even finds a strange solace and self-satisfaction that come with the fulfilling of a ritual duty whose meaning she totally distorts:

She spent the whole night filled with uncertainty, anxiety, and fear, but calm at last returned to her mind. She even found something soothing [*de la douceur*] in having given this proof of fidelity to a husband who so deserved it, who had so much regard and affection for her, and who had just shown them by the way he had received her confession. (337)

The Princess' calm, far from being a victory for her, is an illusory truce. She has overestimated her husband's complacency and is unaware that the scene has been witnessed by Nemours. His presence, as Valincour ironized, "smacks of the novel in ten volumes," [12] but it provides a counterbalance for the Princess' excessive confidence. He has no doubt as to the significance of the *aveu;* it fills him with "keen pleasure" and an intense feeling of pride (*gloire*).

When M. de Clèves puts his wife's conduct back into her own hands—"Given your character, by granting you your liberty, I set narrower limits for you than I myself could prescribe" (340)—he intensifies 'her anguish of responsibility to the point that she again betrays herself. She involuntarily apprises M. de Clèves of her suitor's identity, and when Nemours murmurs some innocent words to her, she cannot repress her insecurity: "In the name of God, leave me in peace [*en repos*]!" [13] More remarkable is, upon the Princess' return to her chambers, the uncanny resemblance between what M. de Clèves now says to her and what she has already heard from her mother's lips: "I see the danger you are in"—"the danger in which I leave you"; "Restrain yourself for your own sake and if possible for my sake"—"Think of what you owe your husband, think of what you owe yourself"; "I do not ask it as a husband, but as a man whose only happiness is in you"—"She begged her, not as her mother, but as her friend, to confide in her all the gallant things that would be said to her."

These echoes are reverberations that penetrate Mme de Clèves and reduce her to tears and finally, in exhaustion, to silence. Here the marriage of the King's sister intervenes, busying M. de Nemours in preparations for the ceremony and consequently providing Mme de Clèves with an illusory sense of peace. This momentary diversion has a terrifying surprise in store for her.

VI *Exposure*

Nemours has imprudently told the Vidame de Chartres of a "friend" who secretly witnessed the extraordinary avowal of a wife's love for another man to her husband. The gossipy Vidame, through the "desire to enlighten oneself, or rather one's natural disposition to tell all to the loved one," as Mme de Lafayette dryly notes (343), has no doubt that Nemours was the true protagonist of this adventure. He says as much to Mme de Martigues, who passes it on to the Dauphiness, who divulges it to—Mme de Clèves.

Her shock is devastating. When the Dauphiness sees Nemours arriving and proposes to ask him the truth of the matter, the Princess very nearly dissolves in anguish. Only thanks to the inspired improvisations of Nemours are they both saved from exposure and humiliation. The situation is extremely delicate for Nemours, who has good reason to think that both women are in love with him. Ever the nimble Don Juan who manages to land on his feet, Nemours at first parries the Dauphiness' direct interrogation and then cleverly plays, through a series of ingenious *double-entendres,* on the Dauphiness' interest in him:

> But I do not know, madam, why you do me the honor of involving me in this adventure. The Vidame cannot say that it concerns me, since I told him the contrary. The quality of a man in love may suit me, but as for that of a man who is loved, I do not believe, madam, that you can attribute this to me. (346)

The Princess has no difficulty grasping the import of this verbal pirouette, and the Dauphiness, opting for the ambiguity most flattering to herself, is thrown off the scent. Nemours' agile exit, however, is badly compromised by his rash decision to strengthen the Princess' suspicion that her husband must have been the person who released her secret.

Mme de Clèves' embarrassment during the agony of this scene is hard to underestimate, and when Mme de Lafayette writes that she would have chosen death to extricate herself (346), there is very little hyperbole involved. (The heroine does in the end choose to retire behind the walls of a religious order, an immurment that is a form of living death.) The intensity of the "shock of recognition" in the scene with the Dauphiness can only properly be gauged within the perspective of the steady movement from the outside to the inside. Mme de Clèves has come full circle from her initial position. To hear the Dauphiness' tale, she kneels down by her bed, a posture she must have assumed to hear some of the earlier tales. The very gesture calls itself to our attention, description of physical actions being so sparse in this novel. One cannot help thinking that here Mme de Lafayette is calling attention to a link with previous experiences. Upon reflection, one can remark that this scene, an example of Mme de Lafayette's consummately unobtrusive art, is nothing less than the *fifth* digression of *La Princesse de Clèves.* In effect, it signals to our eyes, and perhaps for the first time to the heroine's, the complete transition she has undergone from disinterested observer to interested participant. The Princess has progressively moved from an exterior viewpoint, in the first digressions, to partial involvement in the Vidame de Chartres episode. Now she risks becoming "historical" herself, of becoming the involuntary subject of an *histoire*. At the same time that the scene completes the subjectivizing itinerary the Princess follows, it leads her to the verge of finding herself exposed, of finding herself identified in and as *la fable de la cour*.

Once again the frightening prospect of being pinioned between the converging layers of appearance and reality presents itself, obliterating the possibility of *repos*. Moreover, the very privacy of the *aveu* is the only guarantee of its worth to the Princess. Exposure would lead to a devaluation of its sincerity, a truth which is rapidly brought to our attention in the ensuring scene where M. and Mme de Clèves each accuse one another of having violated the secret. Another ominous silence separates them, symbolizing their disunion: "They were so absorbed in their own thoughts that they did not speak for quite some time, and they only broke their silence to repeat the same things they had already said several times, and remained hearts and minds more estranged and more changed than before" (350).

The whole of the Princess' gesture, so sublime in intent and execution, has been voided of its significance. Far from attaining a transcendence of the self (as did Pauline's *aveu* in *Polyeucte*, a source toward which the Abbé de Charnes pointed), the Princess' confession has been reduced to a plea of unsettled sincerity in the face of tremulous self-knowledge. It has metamorphosed into a weakness when considered within the courtly game of seeming and being, a nimble dance in whose execution the Princess has badly stumbled. Indeed, as she hurries from the royal presence, she makes a *faux pas* (348).

The incident has made a shambles of Mme de Clèves' relationship with her husband. He has lost confidence in her sincerity, or rather he no longer believes in its relevance. The incident has also important consequences for Mme de Clèves' opinion of Nemours. She is angered and hurt by his indiscretions and is humiliated to realize that he must know he is loved. His indiscretion, another proof of his vainglory, seems the very mark of his inconstancy. Having fallen from her own perch of "singularity," the Princess now tarnishes her image of Nemours: "And yet it is for this man whom I believe so different from the rest of men that I find myself like other women whom I am so far from resembling" (352). Yet she feels she could endure her unhappiness "if she had been satisfied with M. de Nemours." Nemours is filled with remorse at his conduct and decides that respectful silence is the best tactic to regain the Princess' esteem. He plans to count on the effects of "time, circumstance, and inclination" to restore the situation. (From this point on, the poetics of the glance or look—*le regard*—become a dominant motif of the novel.)

The wedding preparations continue, and as Nemours plays a prominent part in the festivities, he is constantly seen by the Princess, who also has court duties to perform. At the wedding banquet Nemours serves as the King's cupbearer. He is ever present and splendidly arrayed. On the day of the tournament his gracefulness and skill are much in evidence, and he wears colors of black and yellow, the latter to please Mme de Clèves who once told him that it was her favorite color, but that being blonde she could never wear it. These muted gestures, viewed in Freudian interpretations as evidence of the self-perpetuating repression that characterizes the euphemistic situation of the novel,[14] signal the fragmentation of the personality that is echoed on the political level.

When the King, breaking a last lance with Montgomery, is injured by a splinter in his eye, it is the signal for the disintegration of his court's brittle stability, no more resistant or endurable than the vitreous reflection, now extinguished, in which it was mirrored in the novel's opening pages. During the days that the King's agony lasts, decorum is preserved, but the stirrings of disruptions and upheavals are felt beneath the crystalline *bienséance*: "all intrigues were hidden and people appeared to be concerned only by anxiety for the King's health" (356).

The King's death sends the court into a quasi-anarchical disorder. It brings the ascendancy of the Dauphiness and the embitterment of the new Queen Mother; the disgrace of Diane de Poitiers; the return of Cardinal de Tournon, enemy of the Connétable de Montmorency (Henri II's counselor, enemy of the Guises and ally of the Princes of the Blood); the elevation of the Cardinal de Lorraine, who especially hates the Vidame de Chartres.

The significance of these kaleidoscopic changes does not escape the reader who recalls, from *La Princesse de Montpensier*, Mme de Lafayette's contrapuntal structuring of historical event and emotional rout. Like objective correlatives, the frenzied movements of the court mirror the disorder of the Princess' soul, and parallel the disintegration of her own emotional realm. Her relationship with her husband has been altered for the worst: the amenities are preserved, "except that when they were alone, there was a slightly greater coldness and stiffness." And Mme de Clèves acknowledges that the sole presence of Nemours "justified him in her eyes and destroyed all her resolutions." Disorder and defeat confront the Princess, and she goes through a period of despair before regrouping her emotions. This devastation, which affects all the principals, is best expressed by the Prince's jealous outburst: "You no longer seem worthy of me. I adore you, I hate you, I offend you, I beg your pardon; I admire you, I am ashamed to admire you. In short, there is no longer calm or reason in me" (363).

VII   The Night of the Ribbons

Mme de Clèves repairs to Coulommiers, her country house where she had confessed her love for Nemours, thus removing herself from Nemours' disquieting physical presence. In a characteristically oblique gesture, she has copies of several of Diane de Poitiers' paintings transported to her *pavillon*. One of these bears an excellent likeness of M. de Nemours, and it is probably no coincidence that it depicts his presence at a successful siege. Sensual episodes in this novel have not been lacking until now, but to our eyes, surfeited with the easy eroticism to which modern literature has accustomed us, they may seem wholly innocent. Yet within the rigid social codes represented in the novel's world, the earlier scene (of which this is an echo) where Nemours steals the Princess' portrait has sexual overtones.

There is nothing, however, equivocal in the scene that is about to unfold. It is a virtual compendium of the facsimiles of passion, a scene played only with gestures and symbols. Thematically it embodies the drama of *La Princesse de Clèves*, the impossibility of contact, contact which can never be communication, but only complicity.

Mme de Lafayette never describes the pavilion in any great detail. We know that it is more than a rustic summerhouse, for it comprises several comfortably appointed rooms and, apparently, more than one floor. Well-kept roads lead to its setting

La Princesse de Clèves

in a park, and on one side there is a flower garden, separated from the forest by a fence. Nemours is struck by its beauty as he overhears Mme de Clèves' confession, and Mme de Martigues finds it so admirable that she describes its beauties at length to the new Queen.

This is truly the focal place of *La Princesse de Clèves*. In a sense the court is only a pale substitute for the pavilion. The courtly diversions, the proliferation of activities all tend to disperse the attention and *regards* focused on Mme de Clèves, her husband, and Nemours. They are keenly aware of the constant dangers of exposure that the court presents, but they are also capable of avoiding them without too much difficulty. In the pavilion the situation is quite different. The lines are neatly drawn between the forest and the carefully trimmed avenues of the park, between the unconquered growth that passion nurtures and the geometric patterns of a well-ordered conscience. All the images of interposition are here: the painting of Nemours, the fence that separates Mme de Clèves and Nemours, the spy who filters reports of Mme de Clèves' doings for her husband (like his wife, he turns to outward sources to clarify troubled inner perception), "solitude" that is buffered by the presence of Mme de Clèves' maids in an adjoining room, and the supreme denial of contact, Nemours' cane around which the Princess tresses ribbons of black and yellow, her colors. Nemours, who had no trouble arriving at the pavilion by a "well-kept" road on his first visit, now experiences considerable difficulty from the forest side: "The fences were very high, and there were others behind it to prevent anyone from entering" (366). The vagueness of the pavilion's geography is clearly psychological and its setting has a faintly edenic coloring, for it is indeed here that Mme de Clèves confessed her *faute* to her husband, and here that "the eyes of both of them were open and they knew they were naked."

When Mme de Clèves, in disarray and holding a candlestick, moves to contemplate Nemours' portrait, the air is heavy with invisible presences and unspoken plaints: "she sat down and gazed at the portrait with a rapt attention that passion alone can give" (367). Her raptures of abandon, not unlike propitiatory gestures toward the hidden gods of passion, distill in Nemours an essence of joy that atones for all his past rebuffs. His chief enjoyment derives from the indirectness of the scene, from vicariously sharing her *rêverie* and "seeing her without her knowing he was looking." As Michel Butor has pointed out, the power of this scene so haunts the lovers that they cannot stop trying to re-create it, seeking pavilions in public gardens, windows, and secret vantage points.[15]

Throughout this ecstatic night of ribbons, there is a delicate art of silences; the slightest noise of Nemours' sash catching in the French door is truly an infringement that precipitates Mme de Clèves' flight and restores the odious intimacy that she so fears and desires. So important is the unspoken in this novel that its barest articulation suffices to plunge the characters once more into the refuge of ignorance. The only communication here is through the indirectness of a searching glance, a theme already developed in the story of Consalve and Zaïde, whose tongues were of no help to them. They did not speak the same language, but lovers never do in Mme de Lafayette. And so Mme de Clèves who has really no doubt that it was Nemours whom she saw, "thought it was better to remain in doubt than to run the risk of enlightening herself" (368).

Nemours, after his initial transports have subsided, is seized by the unreality of the scene and is tortured by the obliqueness of its revelations: " 'Let me see that you love me, fair princess,' he cried, 'let me see your feelings. . . . Only look at me with the same eyes that I saw you turn upon my portrait last night. Can you really have looked upon it so sweetly and have fled from me so cruelly?' " (369).

Silence, which in itself "says" nothing, confirms M. de Clèves' suspicions as well, upon the return of his emissary: "As soon as he saw him he judged from his face and his silence that he had only bad news to tell him. He remained some time overcome by anguish, his head bowed, unable to speak; at length he motioned to him to withdraw. 'Go,' he told him, 'I see what you have to tell me, but I have not the strength to listen.' " When his man insists that he has no certain knowledge of anything, M. de Clèves almost repeats his wife's thoughts: "It is enough, it is enough; I do not need any further enlightenment" (372).

M. de Clèves is seized by a fever with complications, and his wife returns to nurse him, taking his "iciness" for the effects of his illness. M. de Clèves, for his part, takes her ministrations for "marks of dissimulation and perfidy" and finally bursts into

jealous incriminations of her conduct. He accuses her of causing his death by yielding to M. de Nemours and vows that one
day she will feel the anguish and difference between being loved
by a "genuine and legitimate passion" and by someone who
seeks "only the honor of seducing you." Soon, he adds, in a tone
of bitter regret that suffuses all his words, and to which the
Princess is more sensitive than to his actual reproaches which
she cannot at first understand, she will have the pleasure "of
making M. de Nemours happy without criminal expense" (375).

The Princess is astounded to find herself accused of "sins"
and "crimes," and when she learns that M. de Clèves is referring
to the incident of the forest garden and pavilion, she under-
takes to exonerate herself; as "truth is so easily convincing even
when it is improbable," M. de Clèves is "almost" assured of her
innocence. But it is too late, and M. de Clèves' last words to her
remain, not engraved, for her sense of guilt will distort their
implications, but ever suspended in the innermost recesses of
her mind: "I beg you further that I may console myself in
thinking that you will cherish my memory and that, had it been
within your power, you would have had for me the feelings
that you have for another" (376).

We have seen how M. de Clèves and Mme de Chartres stand
in an analogous relationship to the Princess. The significance of
M. de Clèves' death is virtually identical to that of her mother,
for in each case the Princess is left with the conviction of having failed in an imaginary but nonetheless imperative and
sacred duty. This emotion is particularly strong with regard to
her husband, for both of them, as Mme de Clèves senses, are
parted with the impression of having lacked a full measure of
what, "rightfully" expected from the partner, was most con-
sequential to them: trust, for the Princess; love, for the Prince.
These thoughts sully and poison the Princess' every recollection.
She has not even the consolation of resentment at her husband's misconceptions, which might find release in anger or
righteous indignation. Instead she must feel sorrow—*chagrin*—
that takes the form of self-accusation. There is no end to the
indictment, to what she thinks she should and must feel. She
incriminates herself for not having loved M. de Clèves, "as if
it were something that had been within her power," and finds
consolation only in envisaging future actions "that he would
have been glad for her to do had he lived" (378).

Most disastrously for her happiness, she looks upon Nemours as the "cause of her husband's death," and as her memory reforms and reorders M. de Clèves' dying words, "she remembered with sorrow M. de Clèves' dying fear that she would marry the Duke; but all these griefs *merged* into that of her husband's loss, and she was not conscious of any other" (378).

VIII   Repos

The Princess, on the level of consciousness if not comprehension, is forging the elements of her final renunciation, which will be founded on a global disdain and rejection, aristocratic in nature, that bypasses the uncertain conclusions of logic. To repeat, she disdains logic and aspires to coherence. In the passages just quoted, we can see her preparing a collusion of past and future in order to crush the present. Transposed into moral terms, she is preparing a future probity in harmony with the temporal norm of the past, the "virtuous" and permanent influence of Mme de Chartres and M. de Clèves. The menace derives from the ever-presentness of passion, the frightening spontaneity within herself that she cannot control. In the spontaneous acceptance of love, each moment might be viewed as independent and "sufficient unto itself." [16] This would indeed comprise assent to the maxim that "love is blind." But the Princess' view is not that of a present that engulfs and emerges upon the future. "They lived happily ever after" would constitute a human impossibility for her. We shall return to this point in a moment.

The genesis of this renunciation originates in the most striking mirror scene of *La Princesse de Clèves.*

After passing through a small grove of trees, the Princess noticed, in the furthermost corner of the garden, a sort of shelter open on all sides, toward which she walked. As she drew closer, she saw a man lying on one of the seats, apparently plunged into deep meditation *[rêverie]*, and she recognized that it was M. de Nemours. She stopped short at the sight of him. But her servants who were following her made some noise that aroused M. de Nemours from his meditation. (379–380)

Without a glance, M. de Nemours stands and walks away. This scene is an exact reversal of the pavilion scene, almost term by term. Its effect is to place Mme de Clèves in such a perspective that will objectify, at long last, her view of passion. In a sense it exteriorizes her consciousness, juxtaposing the newfound feeling of a "certain melancholy serenity (*repos*) she was beginning to appreciate" (379) and a violent recrudescence of her love. This scene then dichotomizes the two modalities of her existence, passion and *repos*. The Princess realizes once and for all the hopelessness of fusing the two, still more of harmonizing them. Her renunciation, expressed as the antithesis of her mind and heart—"But this conviction, an effect of her reason and her virtue, did not carry with it her heart"—thereafter pursues its course along that paradoxical binarity of irreconcilables that many readers have defined as the transition (it is really the unresolved tension) between the Cornelian and Racinian ethos. It leads to death in life, to a point, as Serge Doubrovsky has written, where "ataraxy becomes an end in itself, because it is the only way to live up to the Cornelian ideal when one has lost Cornelian will-power." [17]

At the last interview of Nemours and Mme de Clèves, we can see that the pair fails to evaluate their situation in comparable terms. There is a literal contretemps here. Nemours envisages "in the future a continuous happiness and lasting pleasures" (373), whereas the Princess sees only the uncertainty of that future, which must inevitably bring the death of love. Thus Mme de Clèves fears an *outcome,* and Nemours sees only a continuity. This is the crux of the misunderstanding; when she wishes him a "happier destiny" than that which he has had or will have and suggests that he seek his fate elsewhere, Nemours is astonished: "I, madam, seek happiness elsewhere!" But Mme de Clèves has said *fate*; she is really speaking of *repos,* not happiness, which Nemours mistakenly assumes to be her goal.

Mme de Clèves clearly states the nature of her fears, which are inseparable from the nature of love itself, especially of Nemours' love. A future with Nemours would be a succession of predictable uncertainties, for as M. de Clèves long ago explained to her, and as experience has confirmed, one can never coerce another's love, which by definition is spontaneous.

The certainty of no longer being loved by you as I am now, seems such a horrible misfortune to me that even if I had no insurmountable reasons of duty, I doubt that I could resolve to expose myself to this misfortune. (387)

Finally, her ultimate truth: *"I admit that passions can lead me; but they cannot blind me."*

There is a pathetic grandeur in the Princess' refusal, founded on the knowledge that in love only indifference triumphs, and on her appraisal of Nemours' fundamental inconstancy. The very perfections of this *chef-d'œuvre de la nature* insure that he will always be loved by women, and may perhaps return that love. The Princess had already, in the episode of Mme de Thémines' letter, had a foretaste of what that inconstancy would bring, and it is the "greatest of all sufferings," jealousy. Mme de Clèves believes that Nemours will eventually stop loving her, and when she withdraws to a semi-religious life, the passage of time and absence do indeed "extinguish his passion" (394).

Yet we must see in the end of Nemours' love not so much the accuracy of the Princess' analysis as a self-fulfilling prophecy. For it is evident that her suspicions ill conceal fears that she wraps in transparent disguises. (Nemours easily pierces them, denouncing their phantasmic irreality.) There is a lack of *élan* here, of sheer response to life, as well as the incapacity of the gift of self that belonged to the *Religieuse Portugaise*. But Nemours' sedulous rebuttal is unavailing against the Princess' impossibly ideal conception of love. Its very ideality is in the end a means of denying it existence, and one can agree with Du Plaisir that virtue, "far from becoming heroic after long struggles, becomes suspect," [18] and wonder with Antoine Adam if the Princess believes in love. [19]

Her sense of duty to her husband, she freely admits, is largely imaginary (389), and in the following passage one can see that this is simply an "official" motive: [20]

I mistrust my strength in the midst of my reasoning. What I think I owe to the memory of M. de Clèves would be feeble were it not sustained by the interest of my *repos;* and the claims of my *repos* need to be sustained by those of my duty. (388–89) [21]

Virtue, duty, sincerity—these are all so many crutches or stratagems to thwart incursions upon her *repos*. This is not hypocrisy, but neither is it the disinterestedness that these terms imply. It is visibly egocentric and matches La Rochefoucauld's plumbing of love's silurian depths: "There is no passion in which self-love reigns so potently as in love, and we are always more disposed to sacrifice the *repos* of persons we love than to lose our own" (Maxim 262).

Mme de Clèves' detachment from worldy concerns, her thoughts of the afterlife, and her retirement to a convent in the midst of austere occupations precipitate her end, and leave "inimitable examples of virtue." *Repos,* that inward serenity which the Princess prizes above all states, must be defined negatively, as an absence of all passions—love, jealousy, fear—that impinge upon the sanctity of its peace. It becomes in itself a moral value, and its hue, in the last few pages of the novel, is oddly Christian, perhaps Jansenistic.[22] The Princess has learned with Pascal that "le bonheur n'est en effet que dans le repos, et non pas dans le tumulte," but she has not exorcized the *moi haïssable.*

What bothers post-Classical readers is that the Princess' ethical urges are as real as her sexual ones, a state we are not willing to accept. Thus Stendhal: "The Princesse de Clèves should have said nothing to her husband, and given herself to M. de Nemours." [23] We are reluctant to accept that *repos* for the Princess is an ethical imperative which no amount of reasoning will undermine. In the Princess' optic, love is the dispossession of self, and this ultimately is betrayal and not sacrifice. Thus the Princesse de Clèves, through *repos,* attains a moving but uncertain victory, which we harshly pronounce a sterile autonomy. .

In Mme de Lafayette's novelistic universe there are no verdant passions, for with awakening, passion also brings disabusement and desiccation. The fair Princess' final withdrawal is more than retreat, for which we might superficially blame her; it is retrenchment, a truncation and semi-suicidal mutilation of the self that results in that traumatism that goes by the name of *repos.* If, in Mme de Clèves' early demise there is no tragedy, there is a very high dignity, a grandeur that could not exist without some obstinacy, as Camus wrote.[24] Her death in comparative youth seems to be Mme de Lafayette's compassionate way, much akin to Stendhal's in *La Chartreuse de Parme,* of granting a favored character release. Death, for the Princess, blanks the frightening prospect of repentance for passion denied, and of rebellion against the inanition of her creator's summing up: "It is enough to be."

CHAPTER 6

La Comtesse de Tende

Whatever the date of composition of this *nouvelle histori-que*—1664, 1665, 1669, 1690 are all dates that have been proposed—and despite its publication as a posthumous work in 1724, its authenticity has never been contested.[1] It is clearly the harshest work that Mme de Lafayette ever wrote. As such, and because of its brevity (13 pages in the Garnier edition), it is tempting to approach *La Comtesse de Tende* as a thematic summary of Mme de Lafayette's genius.

I Variations on a Theme

We have made the acquaintance of this family of characters and situations before. The heroine knows love and jealousy after her marriage; her lover, the Chevalier de Navarre, has all the ambition of a Guise and the aplomb of a Nemours; the husband is of a rather repulsive character, somewhat reminiscent of the Prince de Montpensier. There are sacrifices, an *aveu*, a husband who falls in love with his wife (a seventeenth-century anomaly that Mme de Lafayette delighted in exploring), and in the end, death takes its toll of youthful error. So many strains familiar to Mme de Lafayette's readers, and yet this little story has an accent of its own. There is a fatefulness in *La Comtesse de Tende*, almost a determinism that its critics have termed Jansenistic, and which makes its presence immediately felt in one of those key words that seem both to concretize and mediate the fate of Mme de Lafayette's heroines. For the

Princesse de Montpensier it was *confiance,* and for the Princesse de Clèves it was *repos.* For the Comtesse de Tende, it is *abime,* the abyss of desperation and total loss toward which the heroine is consciously precipitated by her love for the Chevalier.

The harshness of Mme de Lafayette's treatment is underscored by the suggestive manner in which essentially brutal situations are handled. There is no better example of this than the opening paragraph of *La Comtesse de Tende.* The heroine is married to "the lord of the court who lived with the most splendor and [who was] more apt to make himself esteemed than to please." The art of implication is fully developed here, even in so short a notation. The *litote,* or understatement of the last words is no longer the precious or period cliché which one must so often tolerate in Mme de Lafayette. It is general here, but fully suggestive, so much that the reader, without prejudice, can easily imagine the vainglorious *seigneur* who so casually neglects his child bride and launches upon the seduction of a more interesting woman. And there is cruel indifference rather than prudish delicacy in the paragraph's final periphrasis: "he avoided her presence and no longer lived with her as one does with one's wife."

The Count imprudently and ignobly forces his wife—"for whom he was beginning to have more consideration"—to serve the interests of the fortune-hunting Chevalier de Navarre, bent on the conquest of the young Countess' friend, the Princesse de Neufchâtel.[2] But the Chevalier falls in love with the Countess, and is divided between "love and ambition"; and the Countess, indulging her *amour propre* (400), and unrestrained by any sense of loyalty to her odious husband, responds with a violent inclination for him. The Chevalier's declaration is formulated in characteristically oblique fashion—"Do you believe, madam, that there is no fortune that I might prefer to that of marrying this princess?"—and a telling silence, "more eloquent than words," falls between them.

More lucid than any of Mme de Lafayette's heroines, the Countess envisages quite clearly the path she is taking in thus robbing her best friend of a marriage she has undertaken for love alone and which will constitute, socially, a mismatch:

This betrayal horrified her. Shame and the misfortunes of an affair came to her mind; she saw the abyss toward which she was rushing, and resolved to avoid it.

She kept her resolutions poorly. (401)

These familiar patterns contain important variations. While the Comtesse de Tende is much less fastidious as concerns her virtue—the word is only once mentioned—and more "Italian" in a word (as suits a former Mlle de Strozzi), that is, more overtly passionate than her predecessor (for I believe this tale was written after *La Princesse de Clèves*) she is not as unheroic as might first appear. She is less self-centered than the two Princesses; she can, and will, give herself with a spontaneity that her antecedents lack. The Princesse de Montpensier is flattered to see Guise sacrifice his hopes for a brilliant marriage (as does Nemours) and is totally insouciant of the pathetic Chabanes. And in her confusion, the Princesse de Clèves is uncertain whether her ultimate confession of love to Nemours stems more from "the love of myself than the love of you" (385); it is clear that the same could be said of her famous *aveu* to M. de Clèves.

The Comtesse de Tende has a genuine concern for others; the consequences of love will be even more disastrous for her than for the others, but she will never lose sight of the injustice she is doing her friend the Princess, or the injury she might inflict on her lover's fortune by preventing his marriage. This concern may be socially motivated, but it has little to do with facile obeisance to conventions and appearances.

This solicitude contributes directly to her downfall, for in urging the Chevalier to convince the hesitant Princesse de Neufchâtel of his passion, she is so successful that she falls prey to that "greatest of misfortunes" in Mme de Lafayette, jealousy. When the Chevalier, on the very day of his marriage, threatens to renounce all of his ambitions for her she yields to his love: "Go to Mme la princesse de Neufchâtel, go to the grandeur that awaits you; you will have my heart at the same time" (402). The Chevalier begins to visit the Countess secretly, and not even "perils and obstacles" can temper their ever bolder passion. When he is surprised in the Countess' cabinet by the Count himself, Navarre dexterously extricates himself with all the agility of Nemours under the scrutiny of the Dauphiness, but with an offhanded callousness that strikes a new note. For the most credible explanation is also the most cynical: to allay the Count's suspicions, the Chevalier has only to explain that on his wedding night he slipped away from his bride to visit his mistress, the "most lovable person of the court," and is imploring the Countess to second the flimsy alibi he has concoted.

The Countess is devastated during the course of this scene: that very morning, and for days to follow, she hears the Princess confide in her the jealousy "of which she was the cause," and now she must hear her husband warn, in her presence and in her lover's, that the Chevalier's mistress must be a woman of little worth "to love you and continue this commerce, seeing you linked to a person as beautiful as the Princesse de Navarre, seeing you marry her, and knowing what you owe her" (406).

The Countess must acquiesce to this portrait, for her surrender plunges her from torment into torture. She is assailed from all sides; at the same time that she has "not the strength to disengage herself" from the Chevalier, she is importuned by her husband's newly aroused ardor: "he could not leave her alone and wished to renew all his scorned rights" (407).

II A Singular Heroine

All of Mme de Lafayette's novitiates are apprenticed to passion and learn to bear its anguish, but the wretched Countess alone suffers full initiation and confronts the naked truth of passion received. Her fate, once that "time and circumstance" have triumphed over her resistance, is to discover herself pregnant. Desire is thus embodied as carnality, and satisfaction made stigmata.

We sympathize with the Princesse de Clèves, whose passion is morally disruptive, but we do not forget, nor does the Princess, that passion can never blind her (387). What must we feel for the Comtesse de Tende, a lost soul whose religion brings to her a full and sordid measure of her debasement? It is difficult to assess the meaning of her Christianity. Is it the source of the intensity of her agony and shame, or does Mme de Lafayette thus grant her potential solace? For the Countess is the only character in Mme de Lafayette's works who is unambiguously Christian, and who even has a confessor. Is this ultimate redemption from the degradations to which passion has subjected her? In any event, it does represent a solution which permits Mme de Lafayette to plot the Countess' cruel destiny with a laconism that has the mercy of dispatch.

The Countess entertains for an instant the idea of legitimizing her pregnancy by admitting the Count to her bed, but the news of Navarre's death in the army crushes her propensity for inventing the stratagems that might preserve her person, even her life: "She no longer feared for her *repos*, for her reputation, nor for her life; death alone seemed desirable. . . ." (408) Unlike Mme de Clèves, the Princesse de Montpensier, and Alphonse, whose renunciation in the face of the blighted promise of felicity is typically a retreat, the Comtesse de Tende braves her defeat and draws the necessary conclusions. There is no self-deception, even unconscious, in the Countess, who is perhaps the only one of Mme de Lafayette's characters to realize that escape from the self is an illusory projection of *amour propre*. Thus she alone confronts death, unlike the others whose approach is morally retrograde. They are subsumed into death; the Countess embraces it.

Restrained by "nature and Christianity," the Countess rejects suicide. Accepting responsibility for her adversities, which she admits she "had deserved," she seeks to blacken her living self so that the nothingness of her death may at least be neutral by comparison. This emptiness, which may be filled, is in her eyes infinitely preferable to her loathsome existence. To the insufferable light of self-knowledge and shame, the Countess prefers not the shadow of refuge, but the darkness of extinction. Guessing that her husband suspects a part of the truth, and feeling only revulsion for her life, "she resolved to lose it in a way that would not exclude her hope for the other life" (409).

The Countess, in her *aveu*, seeks no forgiveness or commiseration then from her husband. The meaning of her confession is totally different from that of the Princesse de Clèves, for the Countess secretly hopes to provoke her husband into killing her.

When the Count's suspicions, which his pride (or fatuity) kept him from believing, are thus confirmed so absolutely— "Jealousy and well-founded suspicions ordinarily prepare husbands for their misfortunes, but they do not have the finality that an avowal gives, which is beyond our capacity" (410)— there is murder in his heart and obscure relief at knowing that no living person can expose his disgrace. This relief eventually tempers his vengeance and dispels his first reaction, which was indeed to kill his wife.

The Countess had not counted on the expansive discretion of her husband's valor, nor seen that it might lead him to choose private dishonor over public disgrace (and punishment if he were caught). The Count temporizes, thus choosing quite unawares the cruellest punishment he could have inflicted upon his wife. This is evident from her reaction to his reply to her letter: "She received his note with joy. She thought it was her death sentence, but when she saw that her husband allowed her to make her pregnancy known, she truly felt that shame is the most violent of all the passions" (411). Had the Count given way to his first impulse and killed her, she could have tasted the sweetness of expiration. When this is denied her, she sinks into moral oblivion and despondency; her soul is "drowned in affliction" and loses its fiber.[3]

No character in Mme de Lafayette, save perhaps M. de Clèves, is reduced to such total despair, nor does the author's elliptical presentation disguise the virulence and duress of the ascesis the Countess undergoes. There is no question of derogation from a given virtue in the case of this heroine. She can only hope to accede to a state of grace, and implore that sovereign gift by "embracing virtue and penance with the same ardor with which she had followed her passion" (411). Surely the ineffable joy she finds in death is divine.

CHAPTER 7

Conclusion

"In der Beschränkung zeigt sich erst der Meister."—Goethe

Taine, in an essay on *La Princesse de Clèves*, remarked rather disparagingly that each century produces modes of sentiment peculiar to it, and which become emotionally obsolete through historical remove.[1] The remark has much to recommend it, but it does not allow for a permanence of vision that subtends works quite distant chronologically. For, curiously enough, Mme de Lafayette is much closer to Proust than to Prévost, and a Raymond Radiguet deliberately set out to create, in *Le Bal du Comte d'Orgel*, a *Princesse de Clèves* of the twentieth century. There has never been any lack of titles quoted as novels in the tradition of Mme de Lafayette. Besides those books just mentioned, critics have pointed to *Adolphe, Dominique, La Porte étroite, Adrienne Meursat*, as well as others. (Jean Cocteau made a film of *La Princesse de Clèves*, and Jean Françaix, in 1965, an opera.) But self-sacrifice and renouncement are commonplaces in French literature, and French criticism, ever desirous to frame such themes in a perspective of continuity, has eagerly made *La Princesse de Clèves* their modern fount.

Yet, as Camus noted, the novel of sober unilinear development, the "pure line" attributed to the Classical mold, is really the invention of Benjamin Constant.[2] It is certainly true that the nineteenth and twentieth centuries have felt Mme de Lafayette's impact much more than did her contemporaries, on whom, as Daniel Mornet has remarked, her influence was weak.[3] This is strange. The evolution of sensibility and eighteenth-century sentimentalism were to eclipse her "lesson" for a time, but still it is surprising that having attracted so much attention at the date of its publication, *La Princesse de Clèves* should have had virtually no influence. This is not to say that it did not inspire imitations, but these were unfaithful to its spirit.[4] I will cite one example, that of Du Plaisir.

Du Plaisir, that excellent analyst of the novel, and who wrote, probably of *La Princesse de Clèves*, "far from being biased against a novel in which a young woman would refuse to marry her lover because she imagines she loves him too much, I would be impatient to read it,"[5] concocted a *Duchesse d'Estramène* (1683)[6] that miscarries precisely because it is more of a challenge to Mme de Lafayette than an imitative homage. Du Plaisir attempted to stand *La Princesse de Clèves* on its head, and did not succeed. His title character, a scrupulous and virtuous heroine (whose incessant concern for her reputation is either weakly motivated or blatantly egotistical) with a stern and watchful mother, marries a man she does not love—nor does he love her—while loving another. But Du Plaisir causes his Olsingham/Nemours ("it is sometimes necessary to overcome oneself for the happiness of others") to die rather than his Estramène/Clèves, and faithful to his announced moral— "reason and virtue can form ties as strong as those formed by the most violent and natural inclination"—the Duc and Duchesse d'Estramène move from estrangement to esteem and admiration, and finally to genuine love for each other.

The subject of the novel is clearly taken from *La Princesse de Clèves*, but the treatment is entirely different. Mme de Lafayette's novel is moral without being moralistic. Du Plaisir's novel lacks the subduing and wrenching of passion that characterizes Mme de Lafayette, and Leo Spitzer's *klassische Dämpfung*,[7] the Classical paradox of passion rendered through restraint, is absent. Du Plaisir is only one example that might be adduced in Mme de Lafayette's own time. The eighteenth century, with its penchant for sentimentalism and morality, will further weaken Mme de Lafayette's potential influence. Thus she stands rather isolated in her place in French literary history, more as the end of a tradition than the beginning of a new one. She killed the *roman romanesque* and cleared the way for others to begin anew, but most often they did not follow her.

It seems unlikely that present trends in the French novel can lead in any direction but away from Mme de Lafayette. The concerns of her characters are only remotely related to the twentieth century's problem-oriented consciousness. *Repos* is the very antithesis of commitment; Mme de Lafayette's ellipticism seems laconic and unsatisfactory beside the descriptive virtuosities that, in one form or another (for example, today's *nouveau roman*), have preoccupied the novel since Romanticism. There are no "canvasses" or social panoramas in Mme de Lafayette; there are not even really any secondary characters, but rather hosts of supernumeraries whose functions are generally structural. And the refusal of passion in her works is presented almost as a refusal of life itself. Again, the self viewed and weighed in relation to itself alone, rather than to a group or simply to another, seems an impossibility and a naively limited standard of personal measurement. This is what the seventeenth century called *gloire,* and what we call egotism. Our age prefers to glory in the unheroic, but the loss may well be ours.

If Mme de Lafayette bequeathed anything to the French novel, it was psychology. Psychology is a very old-fashioned word in literature, but it was not so in Mme de Lafayette's time. Then it was not even in usage. She did not write the first psychological novel, but she did write the first one worthy of the name. Love in Mme de Lafayette is a youthful passion, but in each of her novels it kills youth. Analysis is her goal, but in each of her novels the artist's hand is surer than the moralist's, and the characters retain their secrets, their obliqueness, those inviolable and unlighted corners of their consciousness that ensure their human intensity. Psychological analysis in these novels never degenerates into psychologism; rather it dissolves, as the multifarious negations of passion do their damage, into an ethical search of the deepest ambiguity.

The coin of literary worth has changed many times since Mme de Lafayette; her work may not be monumental, but it is nonetheless *aere perennius.*

Notes and References

Place of publication is Paris unless otherwise noted.

Chapter One

1. *Correspondance de Madame de Lafayette*, ed. André Beaunier. 2 vols. (Gallimard, 1942).

2. Holograph signatures attest this spelling of the name, rather than "La Fayette."

3. H. Ashton, *Madame de La Fayette, sa vie et ses œuvres* (Cambridge University Press, 1922), 48.

4. C I, 109. *Bel esprit*, which means "fine wit" and "fine mind," is hard to render in English. The closest equivalent might be "cultured."

5. Emile Magne, *Madame de Lafayette en ménage* (Emile-Paul Frères, 1926). This is the first of a two-volume biography. The second volume, referred to as M II, is entitled *Le Cœur et l'Esprit de Madame de Lafayette* (Emile-Paul Frères, 1927).

6. André Beaunier, *La Jeunesse de Madame de Lafayette* (Flammarion, 1921), 275.

7. Segrais, *Œuvres Diverses* (Amsterdam: chez François Changouin, 1723), I, 86: "*C'est assez que d'être.* C'est un mot de Madame de la Fayette, qui entendoit par-là, que pour être heureux il falloit vivre sans ambitions & sans passions, au moins sans passions violentes."

8. See Marie-Jeanne Durry, *Madame de la Fayette* (Mercure de France, 1962), 44.

9. Loret, *Muze Historique* (Jan. 1, 1651).

10. *Histoire d'Henriette d'Angleterre,* ed. Gilbert Sigaux (Mercure de France, 1965).

11. Beaunier, in his *L'Amie de La Rochefoucauld* (Flammarion, 1927), 72–73, speculates that the *Histoire* might have served as an aide-mémoire for the King when he had Vardes in prison and was trying to unravel the affair of the Spanish letter. This letter, counterfeited by Vardes and the Comtesse de Soissons (the former Olympe

Mancini, niece of Mazarin and former love of Louis XIV when he was very young), was intended to inform the Queen of the loves of Louis XIV and La Vallière, but it fell into the King's hands.

12. M II, 19-20; Beaunier, 259ff. Magne also thinks that Ménage served as model for the Chabanes of *La Princesse de Montpensier*.

13. This work's composition has been carefully studied by Dina Lanfredini in her *Madame de La Fayette e Henriette d'Angleterre: l'Histoire de Madame* (Florence: Leo Olschki, 1957).

14. Charles Sorel, *La Bibliothèque françoise* (Compagnie des Libraires du Palais, 1664), 161.

15. This seems to have been an affectation of hers, for in 1665 she again spoke of her *paresse* (C II, 12).

16. In *Mesures* (Oct. 15, 1937), Beaunier printed an argument in dialogue form that he entitled *Le Triomphe de l'indifférence* and attributed to Mme de Lafayette. Beaunier thought it dated from about 1653. It has since been reprinted in Bernard Pingaud's edition of *La Princesse de Clèves* for the "Club du Meilleur Livre" in 1957. Pingaud agrees that it is similar to the lost "Argument" that Mme de Lafayette wrote in 1663, but notes that it contains a *tirade* from *Le Misanthrope* of 1666. He concludes that the attribution is "fort douteuse" (xxxv).

17. This was Magne's opinion in *Le Cœur et l'Esprit de Madame de Lafayette*. But in another study, *Le Vrai Visage de La Rochefoucauld*, 152, he doubted that La Rochefoucauld was satisfied with friendship.

18. Two pages of proposed revisions for *Zaïde*, in La Rochefoucauld's hand, are in the Bibliothèque Nationale (MS n° 17405, f⁰ˢ 162–63). For the text of these revisions, see Magne II, 140, n.2, and the photographic reproduction facing 144.

19. There is some question as to the date of the first volume. See M II, 147, n.1.

20. Text in M II, 150, and in the third volume of Robert Lejeune's edition of her works: *Œuvres de Madame de Lafayette*, 3 vols. (A la cité des livres, 1930).

21. Text in Lejeune, vol. 3.

22. All of the following quotations are taken from the "Relation de la mort de Madame," 81–91. I have quoted from Gilbert Sigaux's edition of the *Histoire de Madame Henriette d'Angleterre*, which reproduces the 1720 edition. In 1967 Marie-Thérèse Hipp edited an unpublished MS. entitled *Vie de la princesse d'Angleterre* (Genève: Droz). The two versions are substantially the same.

23. Choisy, *Mémoires*, in Michaud et Poujoulat, *Mémoires pour servir à l'histoire de France* (Guyot Frères, 1850), vol. 6, 536–37.

24. Segrais, *Œuvres Diverses*, I, 65. Of the author of *La Princesse de Clèves*, the Abbé de Charnes' *Conversations* (Claude Bar-

bin, 1679) say: "on le voit toujours au dessus de la grandeur de son esprit" (Preface). This is a slight variation of the saying Segrais here attributes to Mme de Lafayette.

25. Mme de Sévigné, *Lettres* (Furne, 1855), III, 315–16. In the indexes of M II and Sévigné, Guilleragues' name is erroneously given as Pierre Girardin de Guilleragues. "Pierre," it seems, was his grandfather's name, and the proper patronymic is not "Girardin," but, curiously enough, "Lavergne." Thus his correct name should be Gabriel-Joseph de Lavergne de Guilleragues. See "Vie de Guilleragues," by F. Deloffre and J. Rougeot in *Lettres Portugaises, Valentins, et autres œuvres de Guilleragues* (Classiques Garnier, 1962).

26. Antoine Adam does not believe that Barbin's *privilège* had anything to do with *La Princesse de Clèves,* and says that Mme de Sévigné's letter is a "faulty copy" (*Romanciers du XVIIe siècle* [Pléiade, 1962], 52, 1358). See also his *Histoire de la littérature française au XVIIe siècle* (Editions Mondiales, 1958), vol. IV, 183n.

27. Beaunier points out that Barbin was not the publisher of either *Bajazet* or *La Princesse de Montpensier,* and contests the letter's authenticity (*L'Amie de La Rochefoucauld,* 182–83).

28. Even *La Princesse de Montpensier* was attributed by contemporaries to Mme de Lafayette *and* Rouchefoucauld (Ashton, Appendix VII, 262). More recently an attempt has been made to place the beginning of Mme de Lafayette and La Rochefoucauld's "belle sympathie" in 1655 or 1656. See Jacqueline Plantié, "La Rochefoucauld et Climène," *Revue d'Histoire Littéraire de la France,* 66 (avril–juin 1966), 209–22. The demonstration is not wholly convincing, as the author herself admits.

29. Marcel Langlois attempted to make Fontenelle the author of the novel ("Quel est l'auteur de *La Princesse de Clèves?*," *Mercure de France,* Nov. 5, 1936). He was refuted by Bruce Morrissette in *Modern Language Notes* (1946), 267–70.

30. See Fernand Baldensperger's article, "A propos de 'l'aveu' de la Princesse de Clèves," *Revue de Philologie Française et de Littérature,* XV (1901), 26–31; see also Bruce Morrissette's *La Vie et les œuvres de Marie-Catherine Desjardins* (Saint Louis, 1947), 109–10.

31. Other evidence of Mme de Lafayette's collaboration is the reference to Huet's *Traité* (published as a preface to her *Zaïde*), and, in the unpaginated preface, use of an aphorism attributed to Mme de Lafayette by Segrais (see above, n.24).

32. This is highly reminiscent of Molière's self-defense in *La Critique de l'Ecole des femmes.*

33. Gourville, in his *Mémoires,* ed. Léon Lecestre (Renouard, 1894), II, 70, claimed that she went so far as to help recruit men for her son's company.

34. Beaunier (*L'Amie* . . . 44–45) thought it dated from 1664. Charles Dédéyan, in his *Madame de Lafayette* (Société d'Edition d' Enseignement Supérieur, 1955), 77, believes it antedates *La Princesse de Clèves*, going so far as to call it *maquette* (model) of Mme de Lafayette's masterpiece.

35. This letter, dated 1690 by Ashton and Beaunier, is probably much earlier.

36. Madame appears to have died from natural causes, probably peritonitis. According to the Maréchale de Gramont, in a letter to her son, Guiche, the autopsy revealed a "sacq de pus dans le foix, qui s'étant ouvert, l'a tuée en sept heures . . ." See Jean Robert, "Révélations sur la mort de Madame," *La Revue de Paris* (mars 1966), 75–79.

37. In French, *repos*, a key word of *La Princesse de Clèves*.

38. Racine, *Œuvres*, ed. P. Mesnard, VII, 106. This letter, from the Feuillet de Conches collection, is of questionable authenticity.

Chapter Two

1. Antoine Adam, *Histoire de la littérature française au XVIIe siècle* (5 vols.) and the same author's introduction to *Romanciers du XVIIe siècle*. Also Henri Coulet, *Le Roman jusqu'à la Révolution* (Armand Colin, 1967), vol. I.

2. *L'Astrée*, ed. Gérard Genette (Union Générale d'Editions, 1964), 16.

3. See Paul Bénichou, *Morales du grand siècle* (Gallimard, 1948) and Octave Nadal, *Le Sentiment de l'amour dans l'œuvre de Pierre Corneille* (Gallimard, 1948).

4. Adam I, 103.

5. "There's hardly any more talk of novels; Yet our people were mad about them." BOOKSELLER: "These days the play's in fashion."

6. See the advertisement of the 4th part of *Cléopâtre* and the preface of *Pharamond*. See also Gustave Dulong, *L'Abbé de Saint-Réal* (Champion, 1921), I, 53–80.

7. *Clélie* (Augustin Courbé, 1660), 4 partie, livre second, 1125.

8. I use "realism" here in its general literal meaning, exclusive of any association with literary "schools," e.g., Sorel's realism, or Flaubert's realism.

9. Second preface (1676) of *Bajazet*.

10. Georges May, "L'Histoire a-t-elle engendré le roman?," *Revue d'Histoire Littéraire de la France*, 55 (juin 1955), 168ff., has noted that in the first half of the century only a few novels are set after the Middle Ages; about 1670, settings are the Italian wars

and the *Ligue;* in 1690, Louis XIII and the Fronde. Settings tend to become more and more modern, and a few novels are entirely contemporary: Boursault, *Artémise et Poliante* (1670); Préchac, *Voyage de Fontainebleau* (1678). On *biénseance* and *vraisemblance,* see Dean May's *Le Dilemme du roman au XVIIIe siècle* (Presses Universitaires de France, 1963).

11. *Lettres,* 88.

12. May, art. cit. The same rule had already been proposed for the epic in the sixteenth century.

13. F. C. Green, "Some Observations on Techniques and Form in the French Seventeenth and Eighteenth Century Novel," in *Stil-und Formprobleme in der Literatur* (Heidelberg: Carl Winter Universitätsverlag, 1959), 208–15. Green wrote: "First introduced by Mme de Villedieu about 1674, this pseudo-autobiographical type of novel, usually entitled *Mémoires* or *Vie,* became the favorite medium of many eighteenth-century novelists." Mme de Lafayette's fictional investigations are clinical rather than confessional, hence the restricted use of first person point of view in her novels.

14. *Almahide* is a novel of the Moors in Spain. Mme de Lafayette will deal with these same Moors in *Zaïde.*

15. Charles Sorel, *De la connoissance des bons livres* (chez André Pralard, 1671), 124, 133.

16. Le Sieur Du Plaisir, *Sentimens sur les lettres et sur l'histoire, avec des scrupules sur le stile* (chez C. Blageart, 1683). *Histoire* is used here to mean fiction. Du Plaisir's *Sentimens sur l'histoire* have been reprinted in a study by Klaus Friedrich, "Eine Theorie des 'Roman nouveau' (1683)," *Romanistisches Jahrbuch,* XIV (1963), 105–32. For an earlier study in English, see Arpad Steiner, "A French Poetics of the Novel in 1683," *Romanic Review,* 30 (1939), 235–43.

17. "It will not be thought strange if in this discourse I submit novels to the same rule as epic poems, for they are only distinct by their versification, and have the rest in common." D'Aubignac, *Macarise, ou la reine des isles fortunées* (Du Brueil et Collet, 1664), I, 144.

18. Adam, *Romanciers,* 12–13.

19. Sorel, *De la connoissance,* 166.

20. Ralph C. Williams' *Bibliography of the Seventeenth-Century Novel in France* lists an *editio princeps* of 1677; if this is accurate, my remark would have to be reversed, and an interesting chapter in French literary history would have to be written.

21. On the whole question of the seventeenth-century *nouvelle,* the reader should consult the March 1966 *Cahiers de l'Association Internationale des Etudes Françaises* (No. 18), in particular two

excellent articles by A. Kibédi Varga and R. Godenne. See also Frédéric Deloffre, *La Nouvelle en France à l'âge classique* (Didier, 1967).

22. Sorel, *La Bibliothèque françoise,* 159–60.

23. Sorel was not alone in this assumption; see Arnaldo Pizzorusso, *La Poetica del romanzo in Francia (1660–1685)* (Rome: Edizioni Salvatore Sciascia, 1962), 49–51.

24. Sorel, *Bibliothèque,* 162, 168.

25. *Ibid.,* 168.

26. Paul Scarron, *Le Roman comique* (Classiques Garnier, 1955), 130.

27. Sorel, *De la connoissance,* 168.

28. On this question see May, *Le Dilemme du roman.*

29. A *feuillet imprimé* of the Bibliothèque Nationale's 1656 copy (Rés. Y2 1556–57) gives this key: Aurélie-Mademoiselle; Aplanice-Mme de Valençay; Frontenie-Mme de Frontenac; Gelonide-Mme de Fiesque; Silerite-the Marquise de Maury; Uranie-Mme de Choisy.

30. M. de Césy? This is the story of Bajazet that Racine was to use in his play of the same name. It is worth noting that earlier Racine had read Segrais' *Bérénice* (1648) in preparation for his own *Bérénice.* I might also mention that Gelonide's tale, "Honorine, ou la coquette punie," is given by Faguet as one of the possible sources of Molière's *Misanthrope.*

31. *Clélie,* 1134–35.

32. See Chapter I, note 25.

33. Gabriel Guéret, *La Promenade de Saint-Cloud;* quoted in Adam, *Histoire,* IV, 171.

34. The *Tatler* (Oct. 22, 1709). Quoted by A. Kibédi Varga (see Selected Bibliography).

35. Mme de Villedieu, *Les Annales galantes* (1670), Avant-propos.

36. *Conversations,* 130.

37. Text in Ashton, 262.

38. Stendhal, *De l'amour,* ed. Henri Martineau (Le Divan, 1928), I, 142.

39. Du Plaisir, 105.

Chapter Three

1. All references to Mme de Lafayette's novels are to Emile Magne's edition: Madame de Lafayette, *Romans et Nouvelles* (Garnier, 1958).

2. For further remarks on the use of negative *pouvoir,* see Dina

Lanfredini, "L'originalità della Princesse de Montpensier," *Rivista di letterature moderne e comparate*, 13 (giugno 1960), 61–88.

3. There are more images of this kind. When Guise enters Champigny at night for his secret rendezvous with the Princess, he negotiates a maze of military obstacles: there are "breaches in the walls" (28) through which he passes, and he must cross a small drawbridge (which the Princess causes to be lowered) abutting on the Princess' antechamber.

4. Lanfredini, art. cit., 72.

5. *De la délicatesse* (Barbin, 1671), 13–14.

6. Georges Bouquet, in his edition of *La Princesse de Clèves* (La Bibliothèque Mondiale, 1954), writes: "Dans cet art tout classique . . . l'état d'âme d'un personnage, la chose signifiée, débordent de beaucoup le signe, l'expression qui les dénotent, à l'inverse de l'art baroque ou romantique dans lesquels l'expression outrée l'emporte si souvent sur la réalité du sentiment" (12).

7. See 414, note 9.

8. "Une faiblesse dont on a été capable à treize ans . . ." (16)

9. Adam notes that there actually was such a Moorish ballet in 1661 (*Histoire*, IV, 178).

10. This is an historical allusion to Guise's eventual assassination, in the Château de Blois in 1588, at the hands of Henri III.

11. Dina Lanfredini sees in Guise "the instinct of a Don Juan aware of his facination; the greater the obstacles, the fierier his desire" (art. cit., 76). Alamir *(Zaïde)* resembles Guise, and so of course does Nemours.

Chapter Four

1. *Œuvres Diverses*, I, 10.

2. *Origines de Caen;* quoted in Ashton, 130–131.

3. The genre is familar to American readers through Washington Irving's *A Chronicle of the Conquest of Granada.*

4. See Jean Cazenave, "Le Roman hispano-mauresque en France," *Revue de Littérature Comparée*, 5 (1925), 594–640.

5. Mme de Villedieu, *Galanteries grenadines* (1673); Mlle de la Roche-Guilhem, *Histoire des guerres civiles de Grenade* (1683).

6. *Correspondance* I, 241.

7. For a full discussion of Huet, see Arnaldo Pizzorusso's excellent little *Poetica del romanzo in Francia 1660–1685.*

8. Certain sentences from this paragraph (which I have not quoted here) adumbrate the psychology of Benjamin Constant's *Adolphe*. Félime tells us that Alamir "n'avait jamais eu de véritable

passion; mais sans en ressentir, il savait si bien l'art d'en faire paraître qu'il avait persuadé son amour à toutes celles qu'il en avait trouvées dignes. Il est vrai aussi que, dans le temps qu'il songeait à plaire, le désir de se faire aimer lui donnait une sorte d'ardeur qu'on pouvait prendre pour de la passion . . ." (175).

And Adolphe writes that in his letter to Ellénore there was "une agitation qui ressemblait fort à l'amour. Echauffé, d'ailleurs, que j'étais par mon propre style, je ressentais, en finissant d'écrire, un peu de la passion que j'avais cherché à exprimer avec toute la force possible."

9. There is some influence of Cervantes' *Curioso Impertinente* here. See David Kaplan, "The Lover's Test Theme in Cervantes and Madame de Lafayette," *The French Review*, XXVI, 285–290.

10. Sister Magdala Grisé, "Madame de Lafayette's Presentation of Love in *Zaïde*," *The French Review*, XXXVI, 359–364.

Chapter Five

1. *Conversations*, 185.

2. *Mémoires-Anecdotes*, 218, in *Œuvres Diverses de M. de Segrais*, I.

3. "L'Intelligence et l'échafaud," In *Problèmes du roman*, ed. Jean Prévost (Lyon: Confluences, 1943), 220.

4. Du Plaisir, our author's most astute reader, wrote that "Nothing falls within the realm of the imagination that may not be expressed regularly" (*Sentimens*, 190), but Mme de Lafayette's interior monologues are not to be confused with the stream of consciousness technique, i.e., the very genesis of thought in its inchoate state.

5. "L'Art de l'analyse dans *La Princesse de Clèves*," Publications de la Faculté des Lettres de l'université de Strasbourg (Mélanges 1945; II, Etudes littéraires), fascicule 105, 288.

6. "La Princesse de Clèves," in *Forme et Signification* (José Corti, 1962), 21.

7. The proleptic functions of the four principal digressions (and the two minor ones) have been exhaustively studied by J. W. Scott, "The 'Digressions' of *La Princesse de Clèves*," *French Studies*, XI, 4, 315–321. At the other extreme, Bernard Pingaud, in his edition of *La Princesse de Clèves* (Le Club du meilleur livre, 1957), very discreetly suggests that the subject of the novel is really that of a *nouvelle*, and that the digressions and prologue may be padding.

8. *Conversations*, 50. The Abbé has confused Anne Boleyn with her daughter Queen Elizabeth, to whose hand Nemours briefly aspires.

9. The letter introduces the earliest suggestion of the Alamir psychology discussed in Chapter 4, when Mme de Thémines writes, "Your whimsical heart made you return to me as you noticed that I was drawing away from you" (310). We must not forget that at the time Mme de Clèves reads these words, she thinks they apply to Nemours.

10. Claude Vigée, "*La Princesse de Clèves* et la tradition du refus," *Critique*, 159–60 (août-septembre 1960), 735. The motif of fate or destiny—the triumph of the irrational— is further present in court discussions of astrology and the prediction that the King will be fatally wounded in a duel, etc. See K. B. Kettle's edition of *La Princesse de Clèves* (London: Macmillan & New York: St. Martin's Press, 1967), xi.

11. "It is not in my character to make a scene: A wife laughs at such foolishness, and never troubles her husband's ears with it."

12. *Lettres. 111.* Even Fontenelle, an admirer of the novel, thought Nemours' presence reminiscent of *L'Astrée: Mercure Galant* (mai 1678), 123.

13. It is worth noting that this, the only mention of the deity in the novel, is purely apostrophic. God plays no role in *La Princesse de Clèves.*

14. See John K. Simon, "A Study of Classical Gesture: Henry James and Madame de Lafayette," *Comparative Literature Studies,* III (1966), 273–83. Marie-Thérèse Hipp has also suggested that in both Nemours and the Princess there is an unconscious search for an obstacle to love. See her "Le Mythe de Tristan et Iseut et *La Princesse de Clèves,*" *Revue d'Histoire Littéraire de la France* 65 (juillet–septembre 1965), 398–414.

15. "Sur *La Princesse de Clèves,*" in his *Répertoire* (Editions de Minuit, 1960), 78.

16. Georges Poulet, "Madame de Lafayette," in *Studies in Human Time,* trans. Elliott Coleman, Harper Torchbooks (New York: Harper & Brothers, 1959), 132.

17. "*La Princesse de Clèves*: une interprétation existentielle," *La Table Ronde,* 138 (juin 1959), 40.

18. *Sentimens,* 101.

19. *Romanciers du XVIIᵉ siècle,* 56.

20. See J. W. Scott, "Le 'Prince de Clèves'," *Modern Language Review,* LII (July 1957), 339–46.

21. After the interview, when the Princess has presumably regained a measure of calm, the same thoughts are rephrased in indirect style: "Her reasons for not marrying M. de Nemours seemed strong to her from the viewpoint of her duty, and insurmountable from that of her *repos*" (392).

Notes and References

22. See Simone Fraisse, "Le 'repos' de Madame de Clèves," (*Esprit*, 29 novembre 1961), 560–67, and Claude Vigée, art. cit., 723–54.

23. Stendhal also believed that had Mme de Clèves reached old age, she would have repented her renunciation: *De l'amour* (Le Divan, 1927), II, 142.

24. Art. cit., 223.

Chapter Six

1. Antoine Adam seems to demur: "*La Comtesse de Tende* has been attributed to her" (*Histoire*, IV, 194n.). But were it not authentic, Mme de Lafayette's son Louis, who lived until 1729, would surely have protested. Bernard Pingaud, in his edition of *La Princesse de Clèves*, asserts that the MS was found in the papers of son Louis.

2. The Chevalier, as his title indicates, is the *cadet* of his family; thus to wed a Princess would constitute a great elevation for him, much greater than he might normally expect.

3. I accept J. W. Scott's proposed revision of *détrompée* to *détrempée* (411, line 29), advanced in "Quelques variantes de *La Comtesse de Tende*," *Revue d'Histoire Littéraire de la France*, 59 (avril–juin 1959), 204–5.

Chapter Seven

1. *Essais de critique et d'histoire* (Hachette, 1874), 262.

2. Camus, art. cit., 219.

3. *Histoire de la littérature française classique (1660–1670)* (Armand Colin, 1950), 317.

4. As Mornet again notes, the pale imitations of *La Princesse de Clèves* are closer to it "in a short summary than in the reading" (312). For example, in Mlle Durand's *La Comtesse de Mortane* (1699), the heroine loves a certain Rucille, but distressed to hear his name on the lips of her dying husband, she says: "I cannot resolve to marry a man cited as my lover during my husband's lifetime." But after many disputes and reconciliations, the Countess and her Rucille are wed and live happily ever after. Another imitation of *La Princesse de Clèves* is *Le Grand Alcandre frustré* (1696), whose author is thought to be Gatien de Courtilz. Another novel by the same author contains some scenes imitated from *La Princesse de Clèves: Histoire du Maréchal, Duc de La Feuillade* (1713, posthumous). On Courtilz, see Benjamin M. Woodbridge, " 'Le Grand

Alcandre Frustré and 'La Princesse de Clèves,'" *Modern Language Review*, 11 (1916), 409–19. In the eighteenth century, another imitation is Charles Duclos' *Histoire de Mme de Luz* (1741).

5. *Sentimens*, 99.

6. Vol. I of this novel bears the date 1683, while vol. II the date 1682.

7. "Die Klassische Dämpfung in Racines Stil," *Archivium Romanicum*, XII (1928), 361–472.

Selected Bibliography

The most complete bibliographies of works on Mme de Lafayette are:

CABEEN, DAVID C., and JULES BRODY, ed. *A Critical Bibliography of French Literature*. Vol. III: "The Seventeenth Century," ed. Nathan Edelman. Syracuse University Press, 1961.

CIORANESCU, ALEXANDRE. *Bibliographie de la littérature française du dix-septième siècle*, Vol. II. Editions du Centre National de la Recherche Scientifique, 1966.

See also current numbers of the *Revue d'Histoire Littéraire de la France*.

PRIMARY SOURCES
(Texts and Translations)

LAFAYETTE, MME DE. *Lettres de Marie-Madeleine Pioche de La Vergne, Comtesse de La Fayette et de Gilles Ménage*, ed. H. Ashton. Liverpool, University Press and London, Stoughton, 1924. Early edition of her correspondence; these letters are collected in the following entry.

————. *Correspondance*, ed. André Beaunier. 2 vols. Gallimard, 1942. The most complete edition of her correspondence. Contains useful *jugements* followed by a chronology and a biographical dictionary. Excellent notes.

————. *Histoire de Madame Henriette d'Angleterre & Mémoires de la Cour de France pour les années 1688 & 1689*, ed. Gilbert Sigaux. Mercure de France ("Le Temps retrouvé IV"), 1965. Good introduction, very complete notes.

————. *Œuvres de Madame de La Fayette*, ed. Robert Lejeune.

3 vols. A la cité des livres, 1925–30. The only complete edition of her works. The third volume also contains the "Portrait de la marquise de Sévigné," "Sur les mots à la mode," and the "Lettre du jaloux."

—————. *La Princesse de Clèves*, ed. Albert Cazes. Les Belles Lettres, 1934. Good and careful edition.

—————. *La Princesse de Clèves*, ed. Emile Magne. Genève, Droz, and Lille, Giard ("Textes littéraires français"), 1950. Standard edition of this novel. Contains Georges Matoré's "Introduction à l' étude du vocabulaire de la *Princesse de Clèves*," and an interesting glossary.

—————. *La Princesse de Clèves*, ed. Bernard Pingaud. Le Club du meilleur livre ("Astrée 8. Collection dirigée par S. de Sacy"), 1957. In addition to all her novels (*Zaïde* is abridged), the text of the *Histoire de Madame Henriette d'Angleterre*, this edition also includes "Le Triomphe de l'indifférence" and the "Histoire espagnole" (on these titles see pp. 13 and 145, note 16).

—————. *The Princess of Clèves*, trans. H. Ashton. London: G. Routledge & Sons; New York: Dutton & Co., 1925. Accurate but occasionally stiff translation.

—————. *The Princess of Clèves*, trans. Nancy Mitford. New York: New Directions, 1951. Fluent translation. The edition is marred by an uniformed and irresponsible introduction.

—————. *Romans et nouvelles*, ed. Emile Magne. Garnier, 1958. Good, handy, and relatively cheap edition of her fictional works. Bio-biblographical introduction and notes.

SECONDARY SOURCES

I. Literary History

ADAM, ANTOINE. *Histoire de la littérature française au XVIIe siècle.* 5 vols. Editions Mondiales (Del Duca), 1958. Vol. IV: "L'Apogée du siècle." A masterful history: erudite and readable. Good assessment of Mme de Lafayette and the development of the *nouvelle historique*.

—————. *Romanciers du XVIIe siècle.* Gallimard ("Bibliothèque de la Pléiade"), 1962. Edition of four famous novels, including *La Princesse de Clèves*. The prefatory essay, "Le Roman français au XVIIe siècle," provides excellent background reading.

BEAUNIER, ANDRÉ. *La Jeunesse de Madame de La Fayette.* Flammarion, 1921. Good biographical study of Mme de Lafayette.

————. *L'Amie de La Rochefoucauld*. Flammarion, 1927. Continuation of the previous entry.

COULET, HENRI. *Le Roman jusqu'à la Révolution*. Tome I: "Histoire du roman en France." Armand Colin ("Collection U"), 1967. Excellent pages on Mme de Lafayette; includes analysis of the novels as well as literary history.

GODENNE, R. "L'Association 'nouvelle-petit roman' entre 1650 et 1750," *Cahiers de l'Association Internationale des Etudes Françaises*, n° 18 (mars 1966), pp. 67–78. Good study of the historical relationship of the novel and the *nouvelle*.

LANFREDINI, DINA. *Madame de La Fayette e Henriette d'Angleterre: L'Histoire de Madame* (con documenti inediti tratti dall, Archivio di Stato di Firenze). Florence: Leo Olschki, 1957. Scholarly study dating the periods of composition of the *Histoire de Madame*.

LOUGH, JOHN. *An Introduction to Seventeenth Century France*. 7th ed. New York: McKay, 1966. Good background reading with a literary orientation; many quotations in French.

MAGNE, EMILE. *Madame de Lafayette en ménage*. Emile-Paul Frères, 1926. Highly readable biographical study. Occasionally reads like a novel, but based on serious study of contemporary documents. Wears its great scholarship very lightly. Includes details of the many lawsuits of M. de Lafayette, and follows Mme de Lafayette through 1661. Second volume is listed in the next entry.

————. *Le Cœur et l'Esprit de Madame de Lafayette*. Emile-Paul Frères, 1927.

MAY, GEORGES. "L'Histoire a-t-elle engendré le roman?", *Revue d'Histoire Littéraire de la France*, Vol. 55, n° 2 (juin 1955), pp. 155–76. Rigorous examination of the relationship between memoirs, history, and the novel in the seventeenth and eighteenth centuries.

PIZZORUSSO, ARNALDO. *La Poetica del romanzo in Francia (1660–1685)*. Rome: Edizioni Salvatore Sciascia, 1962. Excellent and succinct study of the concept of narrative art in the second half of the seventeenth century. Chapters on Huet, Sorel, Mlle de Scudéry, Segrais, the *Lettres Portugaises*, Mme de Lafayette, Valincour, Charnes, Du Plaisir. An indispensable work.

VARGA, A. KIBEDI. "Pour une définition de la nouvelle à l'époque classique," *Cahiers de l'Association Internationale des Etudes Françaises*, n° 18 (mars 1966), pp. 53–65. The best single study of the question.

II. Literary Criticism

BUTOR, MICHEL. "Sur *La Princesse de Clèves*," in his *Répertoire*, pp. 74–78. Editions de Minuit, 1960. On the interplay of illusion and reality in the novel. Importance of pavilion scene.

CAMUS, ALBERT. "L'Intelligence et l'échafaud," in *Problèmes du roman*, ed. Jean Prévost. Lyon: Confluences, 1943. The essay has recently been reprinted in Yves Brunsvick and Paul Ginestier's edition of *La Princesse de Clèves* (Marcel Didier, 1966). Stimulating essay on the triumph of intelligence in the French Classical novel. Equally interesting remarks on intensity and repetition, what Camus calls *monotonie passionée*.

DÉDÉYAN, CHARLES. *Madame de Lafayette*. Société d'Edition d'Enseignement Supérieur, 1955. Good introductory study of her life and works, her literary entourage (Segrais, Ménage, etc.), her sources, the "querelle de *La Princesse de Clèves*." The second edition of 1965 contains a very good bibliography.

DOUBROVSKY, SERGE. "*La Princesse de Clèves*: une interprétation existentielle," *La Table Ronde*, n° 138 (juin 1959), pp. 36–51. Brilliant essay on the "agonizing choice between the deliberately chosen values of an aristocratic code and the spontaneously elected values of passion." The best single study of the novel.

DURRY, MARIE-JEANNE. *Madame de la Fayette*. Mercure de France, 1962. Short and personal, but abreast of latest critical trends. Interesting remarks on the concept of sincerity in the novel and Mme de Clèves' search for inner unity.

FABRE, JEAN. "L'Art de l'analyse dans *La Princesse de Clèves*," in *Publications de la Faculté des Lettres de l'université de Strasbourg*. Fascicule 105 (Mélanges 1945, II, Etudes Littéraires), 1946, pp. 261–306. Profound study of the all-pervasiveness of analysis in Mme de Lafayette's masterpiece. Remarks on the novel's *style pensé*, its use of indirect discourse and interior monologue, its temporality. The utimate mystery of Mme de Cleves' refusal. Indispensable.

_____. "Bienséance et sentiment chez Madame de Lafayette," *Cahiers de l'Association Internationale des Etudes Françaises*, n° 11 (1959), pp. 33–66. Sees in Mme de Lafayette the marriage of a life style and a fictional style. *Bienséance* as the social equivalent of the emptiness of love, its *amour-propre*.

FRAISSE, SIMONE. "Le 'repos' de Madame de Clèves," *Esprit*, 29 (novembre 1961), pp. 560–67. *Repos* and its Christian overtones between 1650 and 1680. It has all the prestige of *devoir*, and even without its "religious aureole, remains a moral value."

LANFREDINI, DINA. "L'Originalità della *Princesse de Montpensier* di Mme de La Fayette," *Rivista di letterature moderne e comparate*, 13, fas. 1–2 (giugno 1960), pp. 61–88. Excellent study confronting Mme de Lafayette's first novel with a work in the same vein preceding it (Segrais' "Eugenie" from *Les Nouvelles françoises*) and one following it (the anonymous *Junonie ou l'Histoire de Mme de Bagneux*).

PINGAUD, BERNARD. *Mme de La Fayette par elle-même*. Editions du Seuil ("Ecrivains de toujours"), 1959. Biographical and critical study with many interesting contemporary illustrations and a selection of *morceaux choisis*.

POULET, GEORGES. "Madame de la Fayette," in his *Studies in Human Time*, trans. Elliott Coleman. New York: Harper Torchbooks, 1959, pp. 131–38. Phenomenological study of the "relationships between passion and existence" in Mme de Lafayette.

ROUSSET, JEAN. "La Princesse de Clèves," in his *Forme et Signification*. José Corti, 1962, pp. 17–44. Fine article combining literary history and analysis of technique.

SAINTE-BEUVE, CHARLES-AUGUSTIN. "Madame de La Fayette," in his *Portraits de femmes*, collected in *Œuvres*, II. Gallimard ("Bibliothèque de la Pléiade"), 1951, pp. 1206–41. Good, lively introduction; uninformed on some points. In the same *Portraits de femmes*, the "portrait" of La Rochefoucauld follows that of Mme de Lafayette.

SCOTT, J. W. "Criticism and 'La Comtesse de Tende,'" *Modern Language Review*, 50 (1955), pp. 15–24. Sees the heroine's rejection of suicide as equally motivated by her Christianity and her lack of courage. Stresses *amour-propre* in motives of both the Countess and her husband. Review of eighteenth-, nineteenth-, and twentieth-century criticism of the work.

————. "The 'Digressions' of the *Princesse de Clèves*," *French Studies*, XI, n° 4 (October 1957), pp. 315–21. Minute and exhaustive study of the proleptic functions of the digressions.

VIGÉE, CLAUDE. "*La Princesse de Clèves* et la tradition du refus," *Critique*, 159–60 (août-septembre 1960), pp. 723–54. A rich and engrossing study. Views the novel as the unresolved conflict between two concepts of human nature (Cornelian and Racinian), and as the ultimate conflict between two irreducible kinds of love: love of self and ordinary, profane love. Remarks on Mme de Clèves' egoism, her fears, the decline of the term *gloire* and its definition in the novel. Lists works of "renunciation" inspired by *La Princesse de Clèves*.

Index

Index